MW00937205

1963
OCEANSIDE
HIGH SCHOOL

Dick Selby

Dick Selby

Copyright © 2011 Dick Selby
All rights reserved.
ISBN: 1461184266
ISBN-13: 9781461184263

Dedication

This book is dedicated to George Mills, as well as to all of the others from the class of 1963 who have either passed on or who are dealing with significant issues within their lives. George was a star football player, champion wrestler, California State Champion in power lifting and an excellent student. He went to college where he played football and wrestled. Eventually he became a lawyer. George is now facing a variety of physical, emotional, and mental issues that likely are a result of those many years spent on the gridiron.

George, you were a shinning light among those of us in this class. You represented something special, fantastic, and you were greatly loved and admired by all. These difficulties that you are now facing are felt by all of us, and somehow once again, even though this is not what you would have chosen, you have led the way. There will come the time when we, too, find ourselves incapacitated and in need of some sort of special care. But our love goes out to you. We remember you, George Mills, as one of the most incredible individuals to have ever graduated from Oceanside High School.

Contents

Acknowledgements

I'd like to first thank the thirteen graduates from Oceanside High School who were willing to share their life stories: Robin Prestwood, Gary Borden, Gary Wilkins, Tomas Romero, Thomas Stettler, Richard Beamer, Jim Schroder, Nancy Boyer, Jim Ghormley, Bonnie Windrich Monahan, Cindy Honig, Janie Quigley Anderson, and Judy Stettler Gabler. It took courage, openness and determination to stick with this project. A special thanks goes to Lt.Col. Lloyd H. Prosser (Ret.) for writing the Foreword.

Paulette Cook Kelly and Bonnie Windrich Monahan, who has her story here, gave emotional support and important information on the various graduates of the class of 1963. Jim Hansen, a retired English teacher from Oceanside High School, provided positive feedback as this project progressed.

A special thanks goes to my wife Barbara who, with her insights and editing skills, along with her constant support deserves special recognition. Barbara, this book could not have happened without you and your diligent efforts all along the way.

Foreword

Lloyd H. Prosser
Lt. Col., USMC (Ret.)

I, too, am a part of Oceanside High School's class of 1963. As I write this foreword it is more than 50 years since we began at Oceanside High School as ninth graders. During the 1950s and 1960s, Oceanside was an idyllic place to live. We enjoyed Oceanside's long and wide beaches, its community facilities, the pier, a newly constructed harbor, the Mission San Luis Rey, and mile after mile of undeveloped open space. Marine Corps Base Camp Pendleton is located next door and my father, like others within my class, was in the Marine Corps, serving in World War II, the Korean War and Vietnam. In fact, he was at Pearl Harbor when the Japanese bombed. Because of Oceanside's close proximity with the base it is known as a "Marine town". However, Oceanside was, and is to this day, a "beach town" and many, if not most of my classmates enjoyed the surf and the sand on a year-round basis.

I remember our graduation. It was held in the early evening, with family and friends gathered at the beach auditorium next to the pier. The sun was low in the sky and there was a gentle offshore breeze. Beams of sunlight reflected off the turquoise water and there was the smell of the fresh ocean air, the sound of crashing breakers, and the backdrop to all of this was Oceanside's pier, extending towards the horizon. It was the perfect setting. The ceremony began with remarks from school officials and from the class valedictorian and salutatorian, and it ended with us receiving our diplomas.

Little did we know what life had in store and we could not have imagined. Through five decades, we have witnessed the assassination of a President and other world leaders, and the continuous unfolding drama of politics and wars. There was Vietnam and the draft. I personally served in Vietnam (1969-1970) for thirteen months as a platoon and company commander. Others from our class also served. We've experienced cycles of economic growth and recession, natural disasters, unprecedented advancements in science and technology, efforts to address population and social issues and the ongoing concerns about the environment and climate change. In many respects, the world of today is quite different than it was fifty years ago.

This book presents the biographies of thirteen of my fellow classmates. These thirteen, representing a cross section, were willing to share their lives and their stories. During these past fifty years, these thirteen have faced the full range of life's challenges: marriage, divorce, health issues, financial concerns, death of loved ones or of one's own impending death, success, and failure. But by the manner in which they have approached life, these graduates have demonstrated they are special.

On August 24, 1967 I married the former Vickie Floyd, a 1964 graduate of Oceanside High. During our active duty years, we lived on the east coast and Pacific Northwest. In 1980 we brought our family back to Oceanside when I was assigned for duty at the Naval Amphibious Base, Coronado. Since then we've both been involved in Oceanside's community activities and the local government. We both believe that it's important to take an active role whenever possible to help, to serve, and sometimes to take leadership roles.

I believe that history will show that as a graduating class we have done our part to keep America strong and to actively defend the principles on which it was founded. I am proud to be an American, and I, like the rest of these graduates, am proud to be a part of Oceanside High School's class of 1963.

Lloyd H. Prosser
Lt. Col., USMC (Ret.)

Introduction

Alma Mater

Oceanside, Oceanside
Can't you hear us calling
Alma Mater, dear to all,
to thee our hearts are tied.
Strong to fight, and fair to win.
On to victory.
Oceanside, Oceanside,
Hail, hail, hail

Welcome to Oceanside High School and the Class of 1963. In June of 2013 it will be fifty years since these individuals graduated. It has already been more than fifty years since they started Oceanside High School as ninth graders. Most of the members of this class were born in 1945 and they preceded the famous baby boom that immediately followed World War II.

According to the school's yearbook in 1963, there were two hundred and thirty-eight graduates and they had the following ethic make-up: two of Samoan descent, two Asians, twenty-seven with Hispanic surnames, three African-Americans, and the remainder, two hundred and five were white.

When this class entered in the ninth grade it was comprised of two hundred and seventy-seven students and the ethnic makeup was basically very similar. Between their freshman and senior years, a little more than 80 percent of the students graduated. There were no differences in the graduation rates between any of the races. These percentages are in sharp contrast to today's graduation rates for African-Americans and those with Hispanic surnames. In the Los Angeles Unified School District, and this is according to "L.A. Now," dated April 17th, 2011, the Los Angeles Unified School District had a graduation rate of 55 percent.

The members of this 1963 class would be directly affected by a significant number of world events and social changes. World War II ended just as they were being born. The Korean War, primarily because of Oceanside's close relationship with Camp Pendleton, impacted many of these individuals and their families.

On October 4, 1957, the first Russian satellite, Sputnik, was placed in orbit. After this successful launch, there was an increased emphasis on education. Educators throughout the United States were concerned that we in the U.S. were falling behind the Russians and it was our responsibility, they as educators and we as students, to meet this challenge that affected our national security and our national pride. Within the schools, math and science were pushed to the forefront.

These graduates also grew up with the constant fear that existed between the world's two super powers, the United States and Russia. This ongoing discord was known as the Cold War and even though we weren't officially at war, everyone knew there was the possibility that it could break out at any time. In the 1950s some people had become so worried about the possibility of a nuclear holocaust that they built themselves a bomb shelter. The Cuban Missile Crisis in October of 1962 exemplified the Cold War threat and it is generally recognized as one of the most serious crises that the United States has faced.

As these graduates walked through Oceanside's campus for the last time in June of 1963, they could have had no idea what obstacles they would be encountering and what dramatic social changes they were soon to be experiencing. The United States had already become involved in Vietnam and though our military force was minimal, this involvement was soon to escalate into one of the most expensive and damaging wars that our country has ever experienced. Vietnam's impact affected the very fiber of our society: rebellion, drugs, the sexual revolution, communes, Timothy Leary, and a questioning of American values. Vietnam's impact turned America upside-down.

I was one of the graduates of this class of 1963 and as we boarded the bus that would take us to Disneyland on graduation night, we were excited that we had completed this most important part of our lives, but within each of us there was an undercurrent of confusion: "What does this graduation hullabaloo really mean?" And more importantly, "What in the world am I going to do with my life now that I'm eighteen and no longer required to be in school?

Well, approximately fifty years have passed since that final bus ride that brought us back from Disneyland. Now, instead of being at the starting point of our careers and college, we have reached our senior years. Many of us have retired, while life's achievements and those accolades we've earned are somewhere in the past.

In this book, thirteen of these class members take an honest look at themselves and what they have experienced over these past years. The stories are presented as they remembered them and as they were told to the biographer. This includes their lives, including some of their family's history, their glory, their difficulties, their loves, their sadness and the wisdom they have learned. **It is**

possible some that of the facts and the specific events did not happen exactly as they recounted them, but that is to be expected. What is important are the events as well as their reactions to them. The thirteen graduates who have shared their personal stories in a sense have separated themselves from the others within this class of 1963 by their willingness to openly discuss their lives. Each has lived through a multitude of experiences and each has developed successful coping mechanisms for dealing with life and all of its adversities. They have faced the most difficult of challenges, sometimes including death itself, and yet they continue to strive onward with a sense of pride about their accomplishments and about life itself.

And perhaps even more significantly, these thirteen were able to provide a framework for successful and happy living that can serve as a guide for future generations as they, too, experience the aging process. This framework will be presented in Chapter 14 as "The Ten Principles for Happiness."

CHAPTER 1

The Military, Islam, Teaching and Life
Cindy Honig

I'm a second generation Italian on my mother's side. On my father's side, I am of German and English heritage, and I have ancestors who fought in the American Revolution. Throughout our family history, as you will see from my story, the military has played an important role.

As I look back on my life I recognize that I have faced many challenges, but even with all of these challenges and difficulties I have survived and been able to adapt. I believe adaptation, or perhaps it would better be described as the ability to make changes in one's life when it is necessary, is a vital part of adjusting in a positive way to the varied and unexpected experiences that life brings us. I think my adaptability is partially because I am a bit of an over-achiever, whatever that is, and perhaps even more importantly I was fortunate to be born an optimist. Beginning with my heritage, my father was in the military and my attitude of optimism I know helped me adjust to this military style of life. As a child I attended eight elementary, two middle, and two high schools. During these many changes from one school to the next, I learned along the way that it's important to see the good and the positive about things, rather than dwell on the negative.

While I was growing up my dad was an inspiration, although I do recognize that he was far from perfect and because of the life he had led in the Army, there were many emotional underpinnings. But I always felt his support and he told me that women could do anything a man could do, constantly challenging me to do and be my best. His encouragement helped me to have the self-confidence to achieve in what very much was a man's world, after I graduated from college, and he strongly believed that I should go into the Army and be an Army nurse.

My father served in both World War II and in the Korean War. He talked very little about these experiences and what happened to him, but others have filled me in on some of the details. He was part of the famous Darby Rangers, a special group of soldiers who were trained to excel in commando types of fighting. Like the Marines, the Darby Rangers led the way in battle and were involved in the most intense fighting. The training he received is still considered to be some of the most arduous that the Army has ever employed.

In 1944, he was part of the allied forces facing the Germans in North Africa, Sicily, and in Anzio, Italy. My uncle, who was also in the Army, recounts the story of searching for and finding my father in North Africa. He told me that my dad was in a tent with his rifle next to him and he looked like a killer ready to kill. He was also sleeping in six inches of dirty water and when my uncle woke him he immediately reacted in a threatening manner to kill him. This uncle was later captured by the Germans in North Africa and became a POW. Yes, you can see that the military plays a strong role in my family.

The battle of Anzio, Italy was especially important for my father. Anzio involved intense fighting with seven thousand Americans being killed and thirty-five thousand wounded. During the battle, my dad's field lieutenant fled the battlefield and my father took over. It was also at Anzio where my dad was wounded and where he was awarded his first Purple Heart. Because of his actions he received a battlefield commission as a lieutenant.

My dad's service career did not end with World War II, but continued in Korea where he again was wounded on two separate occasions and he received two more Purple Hearts. Like many soldiers who had seen conflict in the various wars he rarely talked about his experiences, but he did say the war in Korea was worse. "In one battle," he said, "the North Koreans repeatedly came over the hill and attacking." He had to kill and kill again and they just kept coming. He made statements like "It was not the same kind of fighting that occurred in Europe" and he considered the Korea War as a "total waste of humanity."

Because of his injuries in Korea he was sent to an "R and R" (Rest and Relaxation) facility in Japan. Later this facility was changed into a hospital and while I worked as an Army nurse I worked at this same location. According to my brother, my father sustained an injury caused by a grenade when he was in Italy. My brother has also told me that my father's injuries in Korea were caused by mortar bombings. These mortar bombings sent shrapnel into vari-ous parts of his body and in later years some of this metal would gradually migrate to the surface.

For most of his enlistment, my father was in the infantry, but he did have a brief assignment as an Army recruiter. Because the Army is a branch of the military that moves its personnel frequently, we lived in a variety of locales. Some of the places, like Kansas and Georgia, were hot and simply not the most pleasant, climate wise, and there were a variety of other difficulties: leaving friends, making new friends, and getting to know and be known by the new teachers. On two occasions my brother and I had to take the end of the years tests in schools (New Jersey and Hawaii) that we had attended for only a month or so.

But I have came to believe, possibly because of my optimistic attitude, that no matter where you are and what you are experiencing you need to make the most of it. There are always some good things and you need to focus in on these. I have fond memories of every place that we lived and as I look back on my life I realize I've been to all fifty of the states. When my father retired, deciding on a place that both parents could agree upon required a compromise. Both had their preferences, but California and the city of Oceanside was an acceptable compromise even though it was not a first choice for either of them.

My early education is punctuated with a variety of different schools and experiences, and this is the type of occurrence that goes with being a military brat. During the Korean War, and this was for kindergarten, I lived with my Italian grandparents in New Jersey and I went to an elementary school in which most of the children were black. Later I attended schools mostly on military bases. One of the things that I was cognizant of was that in most of the on-base schools there was a kind of de facto separation between the children of the officers and the enlisted men. It's termed "fraternizing" and I remember once I wanted to be friends with a student, but her father told her she should not go into the officer's housing quarters. My father, on the other hand, was much more relaxed and understanding in this area and didn't seem to mind with whom I socialized. Fortunately, this type of thing didn't occur too frequently, but what did help along the way was that I was somewhat outgoing and friendly, and I was a good student. Being a good student always seemed to make the adjustment somewhat easier.

We arrived in Oceanside in January of 1961, the middle of my sophomore year, but the transition was surprisingly easy and for several reasons. Oceanside High School had many other students whose fathers were in the military, and because of this there was a feeling of commonality. Marine families, however, unlike the families in the Army, appeared to be far less transient. And the attitude in California was more "laid back" and friendly in comparison to Kansas, from where I had just moved. Cliques did exist, but I had never wanted to be a part of this "in-crowd" anyway. There were several students who immediately welcomed me into their group: Mary Lou Brown, Joyce Grant and Rose Mary Kimble. Rose Mary was impressive because she was trying to become a ballerina and she had the motivation to do so. I remember that she would take the train by herself every weekend, quite a courageous thing to do, and travel to Los Angeles to train in a ballet studio, and then she would practice on her own during the week. She was extremely dedicated and knew what she wanted to be. Likewise, I knew what I wanted to be. I was going to be an Army nurse.

The graduation requirements at Oceanside were somewhat different then the requirements in Kansas, even though I was in college prep classes the entire time. My junior year it was necessary for me to take a ninth grade social studies class, World History and Geography. This turned out to be one of my favorite classes. The teacher was excellent and as we covered the various materials I realized that I had been to or lived in many of the places that we discussed in that class.

Anyway, it was because of this geography class that I came to realize that I had an advantage directly related to my father's career. I was young, but I had seen much of the world. I had experiences others did not have, and I had learned to adjust to a variety of difficulties along the way. Dad also encouraged me to use my intelligence and to be independent and I think in many ways he was ahead of his time. He taught me to read topological maps and consistently encouraged me. I developed a sense of pride of him, of the military, and of the family heritage. I knew what I would do. I would follow in their footsteps.

It was at Oceanside High School where my neighbor became my first real boyfriend, and I still consider this relationship special, even though we broke up the summer before our senior year. When high school ended I attended college at San Diego State and majored in nursing. The Vietnam War was going on and there was a tremendous need for Army nurses; and the Army was willing to help pay for my education. This was exactly what I had wanted and I signed up, having a three-year commitment. My ex-boyfriend from Oceanside transferred to San Diego State and during these last college years we were very close. I remember these years fondly and still have a place reserved in my heart for him.

Looking back now, I know that I was young, adventurous, and wanting to prove myself. And one thing I didn't want to happen was to be trapped in a traditional kind of marriage that would end my goals and aspirations. I wanted to see what life had to offer and I had to take the risk. My father had reinforced the idea that I could do anything a man could do and as my education came to an end this was the time and the opportunity for me to prove it. I left San Diego, my boyfriend and my friends, and became an Army nurse and a commissioned officer. I started off as a Second Lieutenant and after three years had obtained the rank of Captain.

In the summer of 1967, I was part of the boot camp in Fort Sam Houston, Texas, with over three hundred newly recruited nurses. Those graduating with diploma degrees from hospital three-year training programs went to Vietnam, owing the Army two years. Nurses, such as myself, with baccalaureate degrees went to general hospitals in Japan and the Philippines, with a three-year military commitment. We first served about six months stateside and then went overseas.

My work as an Army nurse was something that I loved; it was also one where I felt severe anguish over the suffering and destruction caused by the war itself. There is a strong commitment among all the branches of the military to one's county and to supporting your fellow soldier. I felt this commitment and believed deeply that it was my job to serve and care for the injured and to help in any way that I could. As I looked around and walked the wards, I knew that this was where I needed to be and was proud of the opportunity I had to be there, but there was the stark reality of the suffering, and the constant awareness of the destruction war causes to individuals, families, countries, and the world.

My first assignment was in Alabama in obstetrics, dealing with mothers who were about to give birth. This, as my three years turned out, was to be my only happy nursing experience. I was, and this is to put it bluntly, not only naive about life, but even more so about war. I remember in my naiveté writing to the commanding director of nurses in Japan asking to work in either obstetrics or pediatrics. She replied, in a saccharine sweet kind of a way, that the one thousand-bed hospital I was assigned had no dependents, only Vietnam casualties; therefore there were no obstetric patients. She went onto to say that because most of the patients were in their teens, I would be providing "pediatric" care. In a sense, this was true.

This director placed me on the Internal Medicine ward, somehow knowing I wouldn't have lasted on the other wards. I arrived at the end of the Tet Offensive in 1968. This was the major conflict of the war at that time with eighty thousand Viet Cong (the National Front for the Liberation of Southern Vietnam) attacking more than one hundred cities all at once. The number of injuries was immense and as I walked into the hospital it was a surreal, almost shocking experience. The staff was virtually ecstatic to see this sudden influx of new nurses; they had been totally overworked. At first I was working 12 hour-shifts, 6 days a week… and gradually the schedule improved to 10 hours, 5 days a week.

I was single and was dating a surgeon at this time who encouraged me to transfer to an orthopedic ward, which I did. He believed that to really comprehend the totality and devastation of this war, I should be working on this ward, but this was not something I should have done. I can still remember the stench of rotting flesh and the anguish of the young men suffering unbelievable pain. I recall seeing many deformities, and I remember the anguish of these young soldiers as they lay there with their injuries. Gradually the number of causalities decreased and they began to close wards. I think there were thirty or more patients in open bays. (My memory is cloudy concerning some of the specifics and it did take me some time to recall what I saw and experienced.)

My last month in this hospital was on the burn ward. A memory that still haunts me was the sound of helicopters, flying at night and bringing in burn patients. We were the military burn center for Asia.

After this, I was assigned to a hospital at Fort Knox, Kentucky. But to make matters worse, there was a very strong anti-war movement. Jane Fonda and other protestors camped outside, trying to get soldiers to desert. Here on the inside we were dealing with the most difficult of injuries, trying to do our best to help these soldiers physically and emotionally, and these protests were going on. I believed this to be a tremendously callous action. As a result of this, out of fear I wouldn't wear my uniform off the base. I also helped another Army nurse, returning to the States from Japan, to leave the airport and avoid confrontation with these very same protestors. For years, I never openly discussed my military service with anyone, and even now I do so with hesitation. My last duty assignment was the one in Kentucky where I was the head nurse of three surgical wards.

After my military commitment, I worked as an evening charge nurse in a civilian hospital. Seniority was a factor in getting to the daytime shifts and it would have taken me many years to get a daytime position or achieve the same classification that I had prior to leaving the Army, that of being a head nurse. And my placement with critically ill patients proved to be very emotional. I'd seen enough death and destruction and realized that nursing at this time in my life was not for me. There was more that the world had to offer and I was willing to take the risk. I went back to college.

So, with the G.I. Bill providing financial assistance, and working part-time at the student health center as an RN, I went back to school. My husband was also using the G.I. Bill and getting his accounting degree. I completed a Bachelor's Degree in Political Science at Cal Poly. One of my teachers, Dr. Lovell, who I admired immensely, encouraged me to continue my education and to get a Master's Degree in Public Administration at USC. Dr. Lovell said there was a need for more good women in public administration and I decided to follow her advice. I was accepted at USC where I completed my Master's Degree, with an emphasis in health care. I became the president of the health club to help organize the internship opportunities with the various health care organizations and companies. Also, I was concerned about the international students and their adjustment to the United States and to a different culture. Socialization plays an important role in college and I wanted these students and their families to feel comfortable socializing amongst themselves and with others. I worked as a part-time research assistant for my professors. While I did this I knew I was obtaining this education at an excellent university and I utilized this opportunity to the maximum. An internship was mandatory and I completed mine with National Medical Enterprises, Inc. (NME)

When it came time for me to look for employment, my Army experience helped me stand out. It opened doors and I recognize that I also just happened to be at the right place at the right time. A whole new career was unfolding allowing me to be sent into the world where few Americans, especially women, ever venture. I worked eight years for National Medical Enterprises and entered their international division. During these eight years, I made two trips to Saudi Arabia and one to the United Arab Emirates (UAE), though normally not for more than a few weeks at a time. There is an important cliché that is appropriate here: "It's a man's world," and in regard to the Islamic culture and the role that women play this is true.

I was told, prior to this assignment, that I would never obtain a business visa to enter Saudi Arabia alone, without a husband to accompany me, but I did. And once there I was placed in a position where, in spite of the cultural limitations, I had the opportunity to function as an integral part of the planning at several hospital facilities. I was informed that I was the first woman to walk the halls of the Ministry of Health in Saudi Arabia. During the two to three week periods that I was there, I wore a long dress with long sleeves and high collar. It's customary for women in some Arabic countries to be almost completely covered, including the head and the body. It is termed chador and Muslim women do comply.

One example of the role I played was in Saudi Arabia when I was at a meeting with high-level administrators concerning a particular part of hospital design. Because I was a woman I was not permitted to sit at the table with the men, but instead had to sit a short distance away. When the men wanted my input they turned around to ask me the questions. I want to emphasize here that I was in no way offended from this treatment. The way I was being treated is part of the culture and I totally accepted it. Throughout this time, however, I always knew my capabilities and I knew that I had an expertise that was necessary.

I can now look back on these experiences as exhilarating and feel a sense of pride that I was able to be a part of this process. There have been times when I've told others about the role I played and how I functioned in this international company and they have found it difficult to believe. And as the years have progressed sometimes I look back and even question myself. But then a smile comes across myself and I know I was there. I know what I did and I know the important role that I fulfilled.

In my personal life, I met a fellow classmate from Oceanside who was in the graduating class of 1962. He had served in Vietnam and we got married in 1971. He was continuing with his education and eventually became a CPA.

We have two children. Brad was the oldest and three years later we had a daughter, Tina. Tina came down with spinal meningitis at the age of eight months and as time progressed my husband and I were concerned about her continued slow development. She was a loving and beautiful child, but she appeared to be delayed. We had previously been informed that spinal meningitis could have adversely affected her hearing. Out of concern, we took her to be evaluated at Saint John's Hospital. I will never forget the evaluator talking with us and explaining that Tina was developmentally delayed and we had no idea what that meant. We were then informed that our beautiful, loving daughter was retarded. It was a shock that I will never forget.

My daughter, and this in a way seemed to happen almost over night, had become a special needs child and I did what I had to do. I no longer worked for National Medical Enterprises and in order to become more aware of special needs children, and of Tina, I began volunteering in Tina's classroom. I'm not sure how or why things happen sometimes, but another opportunity was about to come my way. We were living in the LA area and a friend gave me an application to enter the teaching program at UCLA. I sent it in, took the necessary preliminary exams, and they accepted me. I was about to enter another career, my third major career, with yet a different aspect of my life ready to unfold. I began UCLA in 1987 and received my Master's Degree in Education. I got a job teaching first grade in Inglewood, California.

Our children were nine and twelve when my husband and I started what turned into a four and a half year divorce. My mother also had the first of two-open heart surgeries and Tina was then diagnosed with scoliosis.

She had to wear an extensive back brace and Brad was entering those difficult teenage years.

We continued the divorce proceedings with my husband being of the conviction that because we live longer and experience more life changes, long-term commitments were passé. My mother had already moved in with us and was a great companion during the divorce. (She moved in when Brad was born to help with the home responsibilities, while I traveled for NME.)   Finally, the divorce was completed and our marriage ended.

I quit my job teaching in Inglewood and moved back to Oceanside. I became aware then that jobs, unfortunately, were not readily available for women over forty, so I worked as a substitute teacher and at a private school for two years, while working on a special education credential at San Diego State University. Then, with the Special Education Credential in hand, I was quickly hired. After three years working as a Special Day Class teacher for first, second, and third grade students, I transferred to San Clemente and returned to the regular classroom as a second grade teacher. Over these years, I taught a few first and second grade combination classes and currently I'm teaching regular education for the fourth grade.

My daughter was placed in Special Day Classes in the first grade and has difficulty with both reading and math. In many ways she is also very immature. I was especially pleased with her high school teacher in this special class and upon graduation my daughter did receive a regular high school diploma, a considerable accomplishment for someone with her degree of disability.

Now that she is out of high school she is employed and has an assigned Regional Center Case Worker, as well as a job coach from Goodwill. Goodwill also provided her with basic employment training, interviewing assistance, and helped her find jobs. For any parent who has a developmentally delayed child, I want them to know that there are people who they can go to for help. The assistance that they provide is beneficial and parents should not give up hope; I have seen the difference that these services make. In most ways Tina is able to lead a normal life. Right now she works at Vons twenty-four hours a week and is able to receive medical insurance because of this. Recently my mother fell and fractured two lumbar vertebrae, and Tina is helping to care for her.

Mom has now lived with me for thirty-three years. She's ninety-one and is alert and active. She has a zest for living that shines and is an example to us all on how we should approach life and aging. My parents did divorce years before my father died in 1979. He was fifty-nine years old. I did mention earlier that he was not perfect and one of the issues he dealt with was drinking. My uncles felt that his war experiences were the reason he drank and he was a heavy drinker. It was not cirrhosis of the liver that was the direct cause, but excessive drinking has a way of adversely impacting the body in a variety of ways and this was what happened to him. I continue to be proud of him and his accomplishments.

I've now taught for twenty-two years, teaching almost exclusively the first and second grades, but there have been times when my past has come back to me. When President George W. Bush ordered troops into Iraq in March 2003, several Marine helicopters (Chinooks) flew over my students and I as we walked to lunch. I became emotional and broke down in tears with those memories of my experiences at the hospital in Japan.

It is the summer of 2010 as we are now talking and I will soon start my second year teaching the fourth grade. California history is part of the fourth grade curriculum and it is something that I truly enjoy. As a part of this, we study California's missions and we have our own Mission San Luis Rey to visit. Also, my fourth grade team has already started organizing for the next school year and I know that when we integrate our forces and work together we can more effectively meet the needs of the students. I believe in teamwork and know that by our joint efforts we will provide a better program serving all of our students.

I plan on teaching for a few more years. Students have a way of making you feel young, which I do feel, and as long as I'm able to do a good job and be happy about it, I will continue. Probably when I reach the age of seventy I will retire.

One thing I believe with all my heart is that in life it is important to keep going and to continue striving onward. I don't believe there is ever a time when someone should say, "This is it." The question I've begun to ask myself is what am I going to do for my next career when I do decide to give up teaching? I'm already making plans and know that my happiness depends on me using these skills and abilities that I've been given. And in this regard I've kept up my RN license and know there is some way that I can combine my expertise in teaching with my nursing background. I don't know what it is yet, but when the time comes something will materialize and I'll be ready.

My philosophy of life is simple: Find the good and make the most of whatever happens to you. Don't dwell on the bad. We're all going to experience the good as well as the bad. Make the most of everything. Make friends and keep friends. I believe it is important to stay in contact with people and in today's age of computers, email helps. Oh, humor is also good. Take time to laugh and see the lighter side, and then with any luck there will be a time when you can sit back and think about what you done, and you just know you've lived an amazing life.

CHAPTER 2

Industrial Arts Leading to Success
Gary Borden

Nowadays high schools have very little emphasis on the industrial arts program and the education that it can provide. I know that this program provided me with the basis for what I would need later in life. Industrial arts helped prepare me to reach my potential and to become successful. Believe me, I am grateful to the wisdom of the educational system that we had back then and to the teachers, crediting several of them not just with providing me with important skills, but with helping me to have confidence in myself and in my own abilities.

I was born in Minnesota. My father was working heavy construction with a jackhammer and in the cold weather this is type of work is very difficult. My parents were ready for a change, and then along came my uncle, Jim Sullivan. He owned the largest furniture store in Oceanside and he offered my dad a job. So without much sadness and with the feeling that a better life was headed in our direction, we packed our things and hurried off to sunny Southern California. I was three years old.

Sullivan's Furniture Store was the largest furniture store in Oceanside and my uncle, who was known for having a few eccentricities, had thrown himself into this rapidly developing concept of advertising. This was especially apparent during the yearly Fourth of July parade. He had a very large "steam" engine tractor that he would drive. He loved doing this. He also had a 1912 Pierce Arrow that was used to carry some of city's most important people in this parade. And because of my father's job and my close relationship with my uncle I, too, was brought into the picture. On the Fourth of July, it was my responsibility to ride atop a huge bicycle, the kind with the extremely large front wheel and the small back wheel. It wasn't hard to ride once you got on, but getting up there took some advanced planning. I had to park next to something high in order to reach the seat, but once I was in place I was off and running. Up and down the streets I'd ride, that is until the parade ended and then came the even more challenging task of getting off. For some reason, perhaps because I'd been riding for quite a while and was tired, this always proved be more difficult. There was a little pedal that was used to climb down, but since I was too small, I would have to find the appropriate dismounting object, which, unfortunately, could take some time.

Thinking back to these early years, I remember that I was the first in my elementary school class to have a color TV. This was sometime around 1954 or 1955 and it was an RCA. It was quite expensive, though I don't remember exactly how much it cost, but we got it for half of what a normal one would cost because my father worked in the furniture store. The outside case was made of metal, but it was designed to look like wood. My dad brought it home and proudly we watched on our color TV, but almost all of the shows continued to be in black and white.

One of my most memorable experiences was when I was fifteen years old. My uncle, and this was because of that fancy Pierce Arrow that he owned, drove to San Diego to meet the future president of the United States,

John F. Kennedy. It was to be a quite publicized event, and I drove along side of him in a jeep, pulling what was a large antique circus organ. It was on wheels and was to provide some of the entertainment. The two of us drove to the airport in our separate cars and I got out of the jeep. John F. Kennedy was there and he came over and shook my hand. This was before he became president. Then Kennedy got into my uncle's Pierce Arrow and together they drove to the El Cortez. That was where they had the big fundraiser and the El Cortez at this time was considered to be the best hotel in San Diego. Even though I realized I was just a nothing, a peon, John F. Kennedy was very nice to me and he was quite friendly and cordial. I will never forget this and I have always thought that he was a great man and a great president.

My education in Oceanside was quite challenging. During elementary school, I ended up attending every one of the elementary schools in the whole city, plus the one they had on the base. Overcrowding was an issue within all the schools, which was primarily caused for two reasons. First, because of the Korean War more Marines were stationed at Camp Pendleton, and second it was due to the baby boom. Baby boom children were born immediately after World War Two, beginning with those children born in 1946. I ended up being bused to a different school almost every year and in one year I switched schools three times. Thinking back on this, however, these transfers actually didn't bother me much because many of my friends went with me. It was also kind of exciting to get on the bus and be driven someplace. I know now that changing schools as I did helped me to learn to make friends as well as preparing me to go into unknown environments and be comfortable.

Because of these many school changes, I had friends throughout the entire city. Some of my best friends were Mexicans. In addition we also had a few blacks, but we all got along. Later, when I got into high school, we had Samoans and they were definitely an interesting lot. Most were very friendly and personable, but you never wanted to make them angry. Samoans are unbelievably tough and that's why our football team was number one. We were so good in fact that some of other schools didn't want to go against us and we were forced to change leagues. Once you became friends with the Samoans no one, and I mean no one, messed with you.

In high school it was necessary to choose a major and I selected industrial arts. I took as many industrial arts classes as possible: metal shop, auto shop, wood shop and drafting. Most of these teachers were good, but there was one teacher who I didn't like. I guess that can be said about any program, that there will be some good ones and some bad ones. However, and this is most important, this industrial arts major provided me with the kind of education that I was interested in and that would serve me best in the future. Most of the academic classes held very little interest for me, but it was in these industrial arts classes, especially auto shop, where I excelled.

In fact, cars have been a fascination and area of intense interest for me as long as I can remember. I actually rebuilt my first engine when I was fourteen and I did the whole thing by myself. It gave me a tremendous sense of pride to know what was happening underneath the hood and that I not only understood the mechanics, but I could fix it. When I was a senior and took auto shop, I even got into rebuilding cars and racing them. This is the type of hands-on experience that helps a person to become an expert in this field and to understand what makes an engine "tick." Two friends and I ended up rebuilding four cars and we raced three of them at the Carlsbad Raceway. Brian Gober, who was also in the class of '63, was one of the two who worked with me. The first car we rebuilt was a 1934 Ford and it was already a racecar before we got it. It turned 127 miles per hour and it won 3 trophies. Man that thing could really fly! The last car that we had was a 1947 Plymouth and we took it to a shop and modified the whole car. We modified everything.

The Carlsbad Raceway, which opened up in 1962, became my obsession and compared to other drag strips it actually wasn't much. It was just a drag strip with a small bleachers area. My brother-in-law, Dick Bocchette, was one of the announcers and over the years many famous people came to race. It wasn't the biggest or the best, but it was a really good time for everyone and you could always count on several hundred people in attendance. I can still remember the excitement of our cars and being a part of it; and I still love the sport of car racing. NASCAR is something that I continue to follow.

Unfortunately, the Carlsbad Raceway has now been demolished and with it has gone an important part of my adolescent history. Houses have replaced it. Most of the people who live in the area don't even know that this drag strip even existed, but it was special and I relish those experiences and I learned a lot. My friends and I raced there for two years, until I got drafted.

Anyway, back to high school. I just did enough to get through. With the good teachers, and we had some good ones, I did well, but with bad teachers, and we had too many of these, I did quite poorly. Mr. Erbe, my auto shop teacher, helped me the most and I still call him once a month. (The date of this phone interview was July 3, 2010, and Gary had called Mr. Erbe just several days earlier.)

Mr. Erbe had a stroke and he's recovering quite well; he's going down to get his driver's license back. When I lived in Oceanside I used to visit him once a month. He was somebody who cared about his students and it was in his class where I was able to put my abilities to work.

My senior year I was a junior instructor and helped out the other kids. That was an invaluable experience and it was because of this that I learned I liked helping others. Mr. Erbe worked closely with me and he taught me to have confidence; he could see things in me that were good and he could see that I wanted to make something of myself. He made me proud of what I was able to do and he challenged me in a variety of ways. Looking back on my life and the various people who influenced me, he is perhaps the most important.

I've developed a philosophy over the years, and I think I've actually been this way my entire life, that it is important to have friends and remain in contact with them. I also believe it is important to help them when I can. I have a friend in Tennessee whose son committed suicide about three months ago. This is a close friend and I went back there to visit and to let him know that I care and to provide as much emotional support as I could. I understand what he was going through and I know how difficult these types of things are. I try to see as many of my friends from high school as I possible and the computer with good, old email, helps me keep these ties close.

One of the most important things I've learned in life is to be responsible for myself and to take care of myself. I believe if you want to make it in life you have to know yourself and know what you need to do to take care of yourself. In high school everyone was trying to do his or her own thing and you had to do your own thing, too. My friends and I got into racing cars and this was our thing. I developed confidence and learned to take responsibility for success or failure. This idea of being self-responsible helped me to prepare for what was to come later.

I was drafted into the Army in 1965, but I knew the Army was not where I wanted to be. I immediately went and joined the Navy. I couldn't see myself being a typical grunt and going to Vietnam. When I took the qualifications test I aced it for both the Army and the Navy. It was these tests that clarified how smart I was and they showed these special capabilities that I have. I was almost off the charts on some of these tests. Initially when I was given my training specialty I was to work on aircraft, but was changed to non-aircraft. I went to Vietnam, but would you believe I never got off the ship. So much for me saying I've been in Vietnam.

I loved the Navy and because of it I've been all over the world. I was even in Alaska for a year-and-a-half and this was something I'll never forget. You could do anything you wanted there. You felt free. You could fish or hunt and there was no traffic. No car jams. No gridlock and you could just enjoy life. The existence there is quite different than in the rest of the U.S. I even met my wife in Alaska. She, too, was a graduate of Oceanside and I'd learned that she was up there in Alaska. My uncle had sent me an Oceanside paper and I read that she'd gone to Alaska to teach. I called and asked her to meet me at the NCO club. We got together and that was how it started. We came back to Oceanside and got married at Mission San Luis Ray in the valley.

After I got out of the Navy, I ended up working for Xerox in Alaska as a service representative. My wife and I lived there for five years, 1968 through 1973. The North Slope was going strong at this time, but the pipeline was just starting to be built. Now approximately ten billion barrels of oil have been pumped out of it.

I would take a trip to the North Slope once a month and service their Xerox equipment. I would stay there for three or four days and the weather was something that you'd never forget. It was cold. At times it could be as much as 45 degrees below zero, but the camps where people stayed were pure luxury. They were all pre-fab and had to be brought up there. The best one, and it was provided by BP (British Petroleum) even had an indoor swimming pool. And the food...it's hard to believe what they offered. The cafeteria was open 24 hours a day and you could have anything you wanted, from steak to lobster. ARCO flew me up there in their own personal jet, an experience that to me now seems almost like it never happened, but I know it did.

There are many other things I've dealt with in life, and as I get older I understand that this is just the way life is. It brings you certain challenges. My wife and I divorced, and my son, who I was very close to, was chronically sick. He had been sick since the age of 14. It was a strange disease and there was no cure for it. I used to come over to his house and take him shopping and just be there with him. One day, and this was about two years ago, I went to pick him up and I found him dead on the floor. This is the hardest thing I've ever had to deal with. I can still see my son on the floor and I think about this everyday.

I'm older now, but in many ways I know I've gone through twice as much as others and what is important is that I've learned from all my problems. I've learned that ultimately you have to solve them on your own. That's where self-responsibility comes in. Others can't fix what's going on. I've had three major strokes and that has changed me. Believe me, things like this change you and test you. I've changed as far as respecting what life is about. You can't feel sorry for yourself! You can't get into this "poor me" attitude. I could hardly walk, but I wouldn't give up. I got out there everyday and did what I needed to do. I forced myself to do it and with will power, pure determination, I got myself walking again. I knew that if I sat back and did nothing it was getting me nowhere.

I've always been this way. You have to have the will to survive. Don't give up! I have a friend who had a stroke and he's just given up. You can't do that, not if you want to recover when life brings you these bad things. And you know what? Now I worry more about other people. I still have many friends from high school and they call. Some of them are just starting to go through it, the tough times. I can see that they are facing difficult issues, but we talk. They know that I care and everything that I've been through gives me insight. It also helps them to trust me. I know what I'm talking about. They call me and I'm here to talk and help. You can't feel sorry for yourself and you have to keep going.

Now more than ever I understand people's problems and I know the value of good advice. When you're going through severe problems, when you're in the middle of things you can't see where you're at or what's going on. Your mind goes crazy on you and you can't slow down. You need to talk with others and let them know what's happening to you. This helps keep you from going crazy. And you need to pay attention to what they tell you. I personally know the importance of talking with others. When life gets tough, talk with people and listen to what they have to say, and always take care of yourself.

CHAPTER 3

Never Give Up
Jim Ghormley

It's amazing how the time seems to fly by, but even after all of these years I have remained good friends with people from Oceanside and the class of '63. Steve Imbilli, Bob Rambur, and Spike Buck and I are still in contact, and I moved away from Oceanside in 1962.

Now let's see... where to begin? I was born in New Zealand during the war. My dad met my mother when he went there on "R and R," which stands for "Rest and Relaxation." My dad was a medical corpsman for the Navy. My mother was originally from England and she moved to New Zealand with her parents when she was quite young. I was born in Wellington, New Zealand in 1944 and at this time WWII was still going strong.

I was in the eighth grade when we moved to Oceanside. My dad was then stationed at Camp Pendleton and he worked at the Naval hospital on base. But it was during this eighth grade year that my parents sent me to stay with an aunt and uncle in my dad's hometown of Ashton, Idaho. I was on the cantankerous side and they felt this would help calm me down and straighten me out, which it must have done. After one semester, I returned to Oceanside. I remained in Oceanside for the next three years, through my eleventh grade. It was during these three years that my father retired from the Marines and my parents moved back to Ashton, Idaho, while I remained with friends of the family. This actually worked out very well for me because I loved my Oceanside experience.

School, unfortunately, was always difficult and I struggled with academics, but I was never a troublemaker and respected my teachers, and you can believe me when I say I had to. With my dad being in the service, respect of the teachers was very important and he wouldn't have tolerated me creating problems. He was military through and through, and in regard to authority he had that military mind-set. You did what you were told and if you did not, you took some very serious consequences.

Now there were some personal issues that we dealt with at home and I know that there were other students at Oceanside High School who were dealing with similar problems. My father had been in both World War II and the Korean War and I'm sure he was affected by what he had seen and personally experienced. He served at Sai Pan, Guadalcanal and Guam. These islands had some of the fiercest fighting of the war with as many as twenty percent of the soldiers being either killed or injured. He was witnessing and personally dealing with serious injuries, death, and soldiers returning to the United States in body bags. Dad, and this was like many soldiers who had been through battle, never talked about what he had seen or experienced, but there were times when his erratic behavior indicated that he was not reacting to the specific external cause, but rather to internal issues that were still affecting him.

I returned from Ashton, Idaho to begin my high school years. This was 1959 and the "Cold War" as it was known was still going on. There was an overriding fear because of the constant tension between the two world powers that we could end up in a war with Russia. And because of Camp Pendleton and the degree to which it was connected to the city, we in Oceanside were perhaps even a little more aware of the implications of any possible threat. I can remember once when there was an emergency of some sort and my dad was simply told to report to the base and we didn't see or hear from him for several weeks.

My dad was fairly large and quite strong, at least six feet tall, but my mother was small, only four feet-ten. I take after my mother and have always been small. Even now I'm only five feet-four inches tall. I was small but compact and very strong. I learned at an early age that in spite of my size I could excel in sports. In fact, sports provided me with the opportunity to have fun, to vent some of my pent up anger that I know I had, and even to become a standout. I went out for football in high school and one of the coaches was Coach Huffman. I respected this coach and have even patterned myself after him. I remember one day we were having practice and I tackled Joe Garcia very hard and Joe was a very good athlete. My hit was legal, but I mean I tackled him hard. He didn't like it and immediately turned and hit me in the face.

Well, I'm not one to back away and we got into a fight, which was against the rules and the coaches immediately stopped it. Joe and I both knew that by fighting we were breaking the rules and coaches made it clear they wanted to see us after practice. That was the time for our punishment to be doled out and they had us running wind sprint after wind sprint. Back and forth, back and forth we ran and they kept asking if we'd had enough. Joe said yes, but I never said I'd had enough. I wouldn't give in, no matter how many wind sprints we ran. I wouldn't let Joe or the coaches think they could break me. Finally it was getting late and the coaches decided that they wanted to go home and see their families and have dinner, rather than continue to have us run. But I never gave in and I believe from this I earned their respect and I learned something about myself. I learned that I don't know how to quit. I will keep going and going, no matter what the pain.

My father retired from the Navy when I was in the ninth grade and moved back to Ashton, Idaho, but I had my friends and was participating in sports. Oceanside also has the beach and I'd taken up surfing. So it was arranged that I could I remain in Oceanside, living with a friend of my mom's, which I did for the remainder of the ninth, tenth and eleventh grades.

My freshman, sophomore and junior years I played football and was good, but another sport was soon to come my way and my life was about to take me at warp speed in an entirely different direction. Oceanside had never had a wrestling team, but in my junior year the school decided to start one and I, and some of my friends decided to try out for it.

When I look back on this spur-of-the-moment decision I can truthfully say that I had no idea what I was getting myself in for and where it would eventually lead. Coach Garrison was our coach and I took to wrestling the way a duck takes to water. What excitement! My opponent and I would square off and the next thing that was happening was that I had him squirming on the mat and was pinning him. There would be many spectators and sometimes they would applaud my victory, especially when I pinned my opponent within the first minute. And around the campus my successes were discussed and admired by students and teachers alike. Week after week it went this way, and I went undefeated up until CIF. Actually, I was doing well in CIF, until my third or fourth match when my coach decided to pull me. I was in terrible pain and had a cauliflower ear, one of the major drawbacks of this sport. My ear had swollen up to double its size and the pain was excruciating and the doctors had to put a tube in it to stop the swelling. That swelling and the complications ended my competition in CIF. It was so painful, in fact, that I couldn't sleep for days and days, but in time my ear did heal and in the future I would again ready for action.

That year was memorable not only because of my personal success, but also because our entire team was good. I was one of the co-captains, and George Mills was the other. He also went undefeated up until CIF. It was an incredible experience to be part of something that was just starting out, and to have the kind of overall success that we experienced.

After my junior year, I had the dream of future success coming my way and could hardly wait until the next year. But the people I'd been living with for the last three years decided it was time for me to move back with my parents and my days at Oceanside came to an end. I moved to Ashton, Idaho, and in my mind, and the way I thought of things because of how well my sports had been going and because of my friends, Ashton was halfway around the world. I would be leaving my sports, wrestling and football, my friends, a girlfriend, and the surf. Everything dear to me was going to be lost, and what could possibly be waiting for me in this far away town of Ashton, Idaho?

My new school was North Fremont High School and in the entire school we had maybe a hundred and sixty students for the ninth through the twelfth grades. At Oceanside we had almost two hundred and fifty students alone who were seniors. After I arrived at Ashton, I went out for football and made the team, playing both offense and defense. And, well, I may be small but I was pretty good and received a lot of publicity in the city's paper. This publicity made my parents feel good because life in Ashton was a struggle. The house we lived in, for example, was actually a converted chicken coop; that may sound really bad, but it actually was quite livable. But money was in short supply for us and jobs for my father were difficult to find. Somehow we made ends meet, but it was a tough go.

Fortunately, I excelled in football, but North Fremont also had a wrestling team and I had within me a burning desire to compete again. Would I be any good? I thought I would be good, really good, but the only way to prove this was to get back into action. Also, in many ways I was still a novice and learning, having competed for only one year. In Idaho wrestling is one of their more important sports and I would soon be grappling against people who had wrestled for all four years in high school. Well, it didn't take me long to find out the answer to the question as to whether or not I could compete. I went undefeated right into the state championships and then I won the state.

In this small high school with its one hundred and fifty students, I was to be the second state champion on their list of state champions. Right now North Fremont High School has more individual and team state champions than any other school in Idaho. This school may be small, but I know from experience that they can compete against the "big boys" in many sports.

My fear about transferring from Oceanside to Ashton turned into an experience that would have a positive impact on me for the rest of my life. In Ashton, I was making new friends, competing in sports, meeting girls, and being exposed to a different way of life from Oceanside and the beach community. In Ashton, it was customary for school to close down for two weeks so that everyone could go out into the fields and pick potatoes; potato picking was an experience I'll never forget. You have this potato sack between your legs and for every one hundred pounds you picked, you earned a whopping three cents. You had to pick a lot of potatoes to make any money at all, but the camaraderie and sense of community was heart-warming and made us feel like we were all working together, which we were. Picking potatoes also has a way of giving you a more realistic perspective on life by bringing you back to the basics.

After completing one year in North Fremont High School, I was now graduating, but what was I going to do? Emotionally I knew I'd always struggled with academics, but I wanted to go on. The unanswered question was could I go onto college, continue to compete in wrestling, and be successful with my classes?

It was at this time that someone from the Mormon community, and we had many Mormons where we lived, talked with me about attending a Mormon college, Rick's College, and joining their wrestling team. He was only offering a partial scholarship, but that was precisely the opportunity I was hoping for and I knew I wanted to take the risk; I went for it.

My first year I was most fortunate and was provided living quarters close to the school. Rick's College was actually about 25 miles from where I lived. However, during my sophomore year I was no longer provided these quarters and moved back home where it was necessary for me to hitchhike to my classes everyday. I can still remember the cold, the ice and that chill-to-the-bones feeling that went deep to my core, but each day as I stood on the highway I knew that this was what I wanted to do. I kept a positive attitude and always got a ride. I did this for almost my entire sophomore year.

Now what happened during my two years at Rick's College was significant, and not just because I was able to pursue my wrestling. It was at Rick's College where I was able to prove to myself that I could successfully handle the academics. Without satisfactory grades, I could not maintain my athletic eligibility. I kept my grades up and in the two years I competed I became a two-time I.C.A.C (Inter-Collegiate Athletic Conference Champion.) This means I was the champion of Colorado, Utah and Idaho. My sophomore year I also took third in the nation among all the junior colleges. I became an All-American, an achievement about which I continue to feel most proud.

When junior college concluded, I wasn't sure what to do next. I was getting older and wondered if I was pursing some sort of a pipe dream. Maybe it was time to get serious in my life and do other things? I decided I would join the Navy and went and talked with a Navy recruiter, getting all the necessary information and with a serious intent of enlisting.

However, fate was to intervene with different plans and the Navy and I were not meant to be. Success in wrestling had not only brought me recognition throughout the state, but because of my third place finish in the national competition three colleges were looking at me: California Lutheran College in California, UCLA, and Idaho State University. My coach from Oceanside, Coach Garrison, was now the wrestling coach at California Lutheran College in California. I received a call from UCLA that was quite exhilarating, but by this time I was married. My wife and I didn't want to move out of the state, making the decision on which college to choose quite easy. I would stay close to home and attend Idaho State University.

It was at Idaho State University where I immediately came face to face with the reality that college wrestling is much more competitive than at the lower levels. I lost my first match. This was actually a good experience and I believe that served to make me even more motivated. But it was also in Idaho where my career took a severe turn for the worse. Twice I had my ear severely injured. The first time it took fourteen stitches to sew it back on and twelve the second. The pain was incessant with throbbing that lasted several days. Then, after this happened the second time, the doctors advised me that my wrestling days were over. If I continued, I would have to have an artificial ear.

Life brings us some important challenges along the way and this was to be one of my most difficult and my most challenging. I could wrestle no more and because of this I lost my scholarship. My desire was to become a teacher and a wrestling coach, and I wondered if this dream of mine could ever happen. I was married and we had a son. We didn't have much money and my son was allergic to milk. We needed formula, which we couldn't afford, but, fortunately, friends came to our assistance and provided us with what we needed. I went to work in the hospital as an orderly; my wife also worked in this hospital. Later I took a job working in a fast food restaurant. The manager of the restaurant knew my situation and would put day-old meat in a sack and take it out to the trash-cans. Then he would tell me to retrieve it because he knew it was still good and that we didn't have enough food to eat at home. I am grateful to him and to all the others that helped us out. I washed cars and then I sold cars, and all the time I continued with my classes. I didn't give up and completed my classes and several times I had a GPA that was 3.4 or better, and I even made the dean's list. I didn't quit. I didn't give up and throw in the towel, and I wasn't angry about what had happened. I just knew that I had obligations and I had to do this. And when I was selling cars I made so much money that I didn't have to work when I was doing my student teaching.

Once I'd graduated and completed my student teaching, I needed to find a job. According to the college placement office, there was an opening in Kuna, Idaho. I didn't have the faintest idea where Kuna was, and I didn't know anything about the school district or the setting I'd be working in; but I needed a job and this was a possible placement for me. I sent in my resume and interviewed with them, and it just so happened that three of the school board members had kids who were on the wrestling team. Well, this was to be both my first and my last interview as they hired me on the spot. And as further good fortune would have it, once I'd started working there they were so concerned that I would take a job somewhere else, they doubled my coaching salary. Kuna is where I ended up staying for next thirty-eight years.

As I look back on these years I know that I wouldn't change a thing. There is no amount of money that could have given me more satisfaction than what I've had. In my garage I have photos of students covering all of these thirty-eight years. The walls are covered with these pictures and sometimes people come back and talk with me about how I have positively affected their lives. Frequently, and I have to be honest about this, I don't remember their names or what happened, but they start talking and I listen, and it makes me feel good to know that something I said or did was important to them. And I'm convinced it's not necessarily what we say that is important, but the way we say it. Communication needs to come from the heart and I believe we also need to be role models.

In Kuna, I coached wrestling at both the high school level and at the junior high school level. In fact, I'm responsible for starting the junior high school program. Our junior high has now won twenty-nine straight district championships. That means we've been champs for twenty-nine straight years. Our dual stats are approximately 388 wins with just 3 losses. In Idaho, we are the school to beat and because of our success people just kind of hate us or love us. I don't think this type of unqualified success has ever been done before in any sport. In 2002, I was inducted into the Wrestling Hall of Fame in Stillwater, Oklahoma.

Looking back on my life, I know I've been very fortunate and, yes, sometimes there have been difficulties, but my wife and I have managed and we've stuck together and worked together for the past forty-five years. We have a "mom and pop" store that we worked for the past thirty-four years. When I think back to when we first got married, we didn't have much and we wondered how we would make it, but I believe those difficult times are also the times that you remember the most and they help make your marriage stronger. The way I see it marriage is a commitment and just because there are some bumps along the road doesn't mean you should give up. Work together. Talk, share, and be honest. Love each other. We have a mutual respect that has helped to deepen this relationship and our love. We have two lovely children and three grandchildren, and we both love being grandparents. I think God had a reason for making us grandparents. We are free to spoil these kids, just love them, and we are also in a position to help provide them money for college.

When I look back on my life I know it has been amazing and that I've achieved my wildest dreams. I was just a scrawny little kid who liked sports, didn't particularly like academics, but I know that I would never give up.

I wasn't great with my studies, especially early on, but I didn't let that stop me. I kept going and people helped me all along the way. I think if there is a secret to life, success, and happiness it's this: Keep going. Don't give up and when you get the chance, do what you can to help others.

CHAPTER 4

Courage
Bonnie Windrich Monahan

Over the past years, I believe it could be said that I'm an Oceanside Pirate through and through. I try to keep in touch with as many of my classmates as I can, and our class reunions are very important to me. I know that some of my classmates have passed on, and that many of us are dealing with a variety of unexpected events and circumstances. I, too, have been facing some unforeseen setbacks, but the important thing for me now is to keep focused on my goal and continue doing the necessary physical therapy exercises. For approximately two years, I've been mostly confined to a wheelchair, unable to walk, but this is changing. I'll explain more about this later, but first to my genealogy, of which I have a great interest and which relates directly to my attitudes and how I live my life.

Both of my maternal grandparents came from Ireland, with my grandfather immigrating to the United Sates at the age of twenty-five in 1914. For my grandfather, once he got here he initiated a slow process of family unification and integration. First, he brought over his childhood sweetheart, who later became his wife. Then he brought over the other relatives. One of the issues they were dealing with was Ireland's struggle for independence from

England. There had been open hostilities between the two countries for about a hundred and fifty years. In fact, my grandfather's two brothers were directly involved in this fighting. One was shot in the leg and it had to be amputated.

The other factor leading to my grandparents' immigration dealt with agriculture. Ireland had experienced wide spread famine from what was an almost complete devastation of the potato crop, their primary mainstay, and approximately one million people had died. One thing my grandfather did, and this was during the Great Depression, was to supply everyone who needed it within his neighborhood with food. He was employed as a fireman, and helping others was a part of his philosophy.

When I think back to my childhood I have the fondest memories of my grandfather taking me for walks during the winter months, pulling me on my little sled. I played in the snow and felt so happy and special, and as I played my grandfather was teaching. He knew that to survive you had to be tough and he was instilling in me the toughness that I would need in life. His values about how to live, how to save, helping others, and how to keep striving onward, no matter what happens, became my values.

And now to my father: He was in the Marine Corps during World War II and then became a career Marine. During the war, he did most of his fighting in the South Pacific and was at Iwo Jima. Iwo Jima was one of the most intense battles of the war. Almost seven thousand Americans were killed and eighteen thousand were wounded. Twenty-two thousand Japanese were on the island and all but approximately two hundred died. Many of those were killed in action while others, from a loss of self-respect for losing this battle and this island, killed themselves.

World War II ended in 1945, the year I was born. My real name is Alita Marie, but my grandfather disliked this name so he nicknamed me Bonnie. Almost immediately after I was born my parents divorced, with my father choosing a military career over marriage and family. According to the information I've been given, the emphasis in the Marine Corps immediately after World War II was for their soldiers to be single. This may have had something to do with the number of casualties experienced during the war, believing that it might make for a more proficient fighting force. Four years later, however, the unexpected happened. My dad was stationed at Camp Pendleton and he called my mother to see if we would come out for a short vacation to visit him. Well, that brief trip led to them being remarried in 1949, with us remaining with him in the Oceanside/ Carlsbad area. At first we lived in North Oceanside and were within easy walking distance of the beach. I remember daring myself to explore an abandoned trailer, which I'd passed many times before. I carefully moved around the various interior objects, thinking that this trailer might have recently have been used. I was a gutsy little kid. I was to learn several days later that I'd been exposed to lice, as well as the harshness of my father's homespun remedy. He put kerosene in my hair and placed me in the shower to wash it off. He gently washed my head of all the harsh chemicals, but didn't realize the deleterious affects that this remedy would have. Much of my hair fell out, an experience I have never forgotten.

We later moved to Carlsbad, a preferred location. There were many open spaces, with hills covered with brush and the beach was relatively close. Our house was one of three located near the top of a hill overlooking the lagoon, the bird sanctuary that serves to separate Carlsbad from South Oceanside. My father, who was independently minded, constructed a chicken coop so we could have fresh eggs and chicken whenever we wanted. His desire to maintain a sense of independence, along with his semi-honed skills in basic carpentry, played an important role for us in the near future.

In June of 1950, the Korean War broke out and my father was among the first to be deployed. The Korean War, for those who'd experienced both World War II and Korea, was considered to be much more horrific. The fighting was intense and the weather conditions were intolerable. After his deployment, he had a dream, a kind of premonition that he would not be returning, and this dream turned out to be reality. He did not return, having been killed in action. Posthumously, he received the "Congressional Medal of Honor," the most distinguished medal that can be presented to anyone in the military that earned it.

This is the citation that was presented along with his Medal of Honor:

Medal of Honor citation
The President of the United States in the name of The Congress takes pride in presenting the MEDAL OF HONOR posthumously to

STAFF SERGEANT WILLIAM G. WINDRICH

UNITED STATES MARINE CORPS

for service as set forth in the following CITATION:

For conspicuous gallantry and intrepidity at the risk of his life above and beyond the call of duty as Platoon Sergeant of Company I, Third Battalion, Fifth Marines, First

Marine Division (Reinforced), in action against enemy aggressor forces in the vicinity of Yudam-ni, Korea, the night of 1 December 1950. Promptly organizing a squad of men when the enemy launched a sudden, vicious counterattack against the forward elements of his company's position, rendering it untenable, Staff Sergeant Windrich, armed with a carbine, spearheaded the assault to the top of the knoll immediately confronting the overwhelming force and, under shattering hostile automatic weapons, mortar and grenade fire, directed effective fire to hold back the attackers and cover the withdrawal of our troops to commanding ground. With seven of his men struck down during the furious action and he, himself, wounded in the head by a bursting grenade, he made his way to his company's position and, organizing a small group of volunteers, returned with them to evacuate the wounded and dying form the frozen hillside, staunchly refusing medical attention himself. Immediately redeploying the remainder of his troops, Staff Sergeant Windrich placed them on the left flank of the defensive sector before the enemy again attacked in force. Wounded in the leg during the bitter fight that followed, he bravely fought on with his men, shouting words of encouragement and directing their fire until the attack was repelled. Refusing evacuation although unable to stand, he still continued to direct his platoon in setting up defensive positions until, weakened by the bitter cold, excessive loss of blood and severe pain, he lapsed into unconsciousness and died. His valiant leadership, fortitude and courageous fighting spirit against tremendous odds served to inspire others to heroic endeavor in holding the objective and reflect the highest credit upon Staff Sergeant Windrich and the United States Naval Service. He gallantly gave his life for his country.
/S/ HARRY S. TRUMAN

Immediately following my father's death we found ourselves abandoned by the United States government. Though we had been informed that he had been killed in action, there was no actual body from which to make the final confirmation. There were thousands of other soldiers who had also been killed, but their bodies, too, remained in Korea. A book by W.E.B. Griffin titled, *Retreat Hell*, describes this battle. Some of the dead and wounded were tied onto trucks so that they could be transported out. But many of the soldiers who were not brought back were simply placed into holes or caverns in the surrounding hills, which was what had happened with my father.

With no assistance from the government, we were then forced to go many months without any income. My aunt, an unemployed nurse, was living with us just before my father was deployed. My mother was an unemployed waitress and we now found ourselves destitute. Though I was only five years old, I can still remember walking the streets and hills on the way to town with my aunt searching for soda and beer bottles so that we could redeem them at a nearby store. This money was used to purchase a giant bag of black-eyed peas. We then brought these beans home. Next Aunt Jo killed a chicken and together we would pluck and clean it. When my mother arrived home, after trying to find work, it was her task to do the cooking. We ate this food and believed that the only reason we were able to survive during this difficult period was because of my father's insistence on having this chicken coop. I still hate black-eyed peas.

As a result of my own personal experiences I know that war is hell, and not just because of the devastation to those directly involved, but to those indirectly involved. For my mother and me, it would be approximately five years until thousands of these soldiers' bodies were transported from Korea to Kokura, Japan. My father, out of the thousands who were returned from Korea, was to be the only one positively identified. This identification occurred in Kokura, both through his dental records and because of his physical characteristics. His body was then returned to the United States and he was buried in Arlington National Cemetery 29 July 1955. The remains of the other thousands of soldiers were buried in Hawaii.

These difficulties, and they were tremendous, brought us closer together as a family. I also know that from what I experienced I was becoming knowledgeable of the important survival skills. I was developing a deep respect for self-sufficiency and of never letting myself somehow fall into a position where I could be trapped. My grandfather's teachings also would not be forgotten. But through these experiences something else was happening. I learned compassion. I know what it's like to be down and out and to have your life collapse overnight. It can happen to anyone and I've developed the deepest feeling for others who find themselves, through no fault of their own, in this situation.

My mother remarried when I was nine, marrying another Marine and we moved to North Carolina where I attended school for two years. Then it was back to Oceanside and South Oceanside Elementary School where an education of a different kind was about to begin.

Because of overcrowding my sixth grade class was sent to the other side of town, Laurel Street School. Here we found ourselves in what was a new and unexpected situation. We, from South Oceanside, had become the minorities among their majority, Mexican and African-American. The integration process in Oceanside was hard at work long before it was to become a national mandate. But there were some unexpected stumbling blocks along the way and I was to experience one first hand. I was accosted by a group of Mexican girls. They yanked me off the bus, pushing and hitting me, with no one coming to my assistance. I believe that the supervision was very inadequate at this time. Later I was to learn the reason for my treatment. I had done the unthinkable and invaded their turf.

This was a terrifying experience, though this was to be my secret and mine alone. That sixth grade year ended and Laurel Street School and its de facto integration were now behind us. Interestingly enough, years later and at our ten-year class reunion these Mexican girls and I became friends. At this time, however, it was almost sixteen years after they had pulled me off the bus, but at last we were able to joke about what had happened. It was a tough way to learn, but I've come to believe that in the long run it was positive. It was at Laurel Street School where we whites were getting an education about how another part of the world functions, and we were learning from our real-life experiences.

Let's now make the big move and get into high school. In 1959 there was a kind of ritual at Oceanside High School that ninth graders as the incoming lower classmen were to be harassed by their senior counterparts. The official term for this is "hazing" and nowadays it's not just controversial, but also illegal. In 1959, however, it was almost an expected part of the ninth graders matriculation. It was the custom for ninth grade boys to have their hair cut very short by an upperclassman, while the girls were usually subjected to perform some sort of menial task. Once I began the ninth grade it wasn't long before I learned my role. I was to carry books for a senior boy. He was feisty, to say the least, with a bit of an attitude. I was his personal helper, lugging books from one class to the next, and then rushing off to my own, hoping I wouldn't be late. I thanked God when this requirement was satisfied and there would be no more of these unsanctioned and undesired ninth grade obligations.

My education was then able to progress in a somewhat normal fashion, if there is such a thing, except I was rebellious... a trait I'd inherited from my father. I wasn't particularly interested in school or those constrictive, perhaps even ridiculous, rules that were imposed upon us. In many ways I was an early representation of those rebellious "sixties" that were just on the horizon. I remember the time I'd been ditching with a friend, having gone out to what was termed the "dunes." Oceanside's marina is now there and Mr. Brennaman, the truant officer, was hot on our trail. We ran, hoping to escape detection. Crossing the freeway, we skidded around an obscure corner at a gas station and carefully slipped into the girl's bathroom. Breathing heavily and hearts beating rapidly, we were sure we'd beaten his watchful eye, only to find ourselves called into the vice-principal's office the following day.

Mrs. Morse was the girls' vice principal and meetings with her meant you were in big trouble. She was probably around six feet tall and during our initial conferences I know I felt quite intimidated. Later, however, after a variety of cause and effect meetings--me being the cause and she being the effect--I came to respect her and to know that she wanted the best for me; but wanting the best is one thing, change is another. I, being only minimally deterred by her ever-watchful eye, continued my patterns of non-compliance.

Fortunately, my senior year arrived and with this came what I would term as a transformation. "I'm going to soon graduate," I said to myself and it came as a kind of revelation. I realized that it would not be long until I was released into another world. A place where I would no longer be required to attend classes, listen to teachers, or do homework. I settled down, got my act together, and slowly eased into becoming what I am today, a life-long Pirate.

It was during my freshman year that I took a class that was to have a dramatic effect on me. It was a crafts class where we worked with clay. I had taken it primarily because I'd enjoyed working with clay as a child. I'd thought to myself... *This sounds like fun*, but it proved to be a real struggle. I was like a duck out of water, waddling along, but when it ended I went out and purchased some art supplies and a new kind of life was beginning.

It was slow going, but I didn't give up. I went from the basics and stick figures to replicating photographs, and painting them exactly as in the photograph I had taken. I learned as I progressed not to put specific limits on myself, but to let this inside potential flow naturally. And perhaps even more importantly, I was gaining a tremendous appreciation of the beauty surrounding me. I was now seeing the world through the eyes of an artist. Then I discovered that I could take a photograph and improvise my visions into a painting and create something new and original. Photography, an adjunct to my artwork, became another interest and little did I know the role that this would play later in my life. I purchased a good camera and learned to develop my own pictures. In a short time I even had my own dark room. I enjoyed the excitement and the challenges, and was doing all of this entirely on my own.

I met my husband when I was in high school, around the age of sixteen. We dated for five and one-half years and married when I was twenty-one. By this time he'd been drafted into the Army. The marriage lasted for almost fifteen years. Looking back on these fifteen years, one of the most important aspects was that we lived in Germany for two and one-half years. Residing in Germany meant living with another language and meeting people from different cultures, and each day we experienced the novel and the unexpected. I learned the language. We enjoyed the *Oktoberfest* and its big parade, plus we traveled throughout Western Europe, loving every second of it. The idea of seeing other places and people had formed a solid base within my psyche. I would never be the same.

My husband and I have gone our own separate ways. We had a son after we'd been married for ten years. It was important to me that when we divorced that we dissolved the marriage with minimal amounts of anger, which we did. I was concerned about our son as he was the number one person in my life. Because of our mutual concern for his best interests, both of us were able to remain good friends.

There were many adjustments to be made in my life once I was again single, and I found I enjoyed the freedom. For a while it was a wild and crazy time, but the writing was on the wall for me to take a good look at myself. My life was not what I wanted and another change was on its way.

In 1985 my son and I were living in Orange County. I'd been single for several years and my apartment was broken into and it was worse than what you see in the movies. And on top of this my son, Mark, had witnessed a murder. It was gang related and we were told that his life was now in danger. I was suddenly faced with an important decision: remaining in Orange County, but in a different location, or moving away from Orange County. If I decided to move, there were several places that I had in mind, but Oceanside was my first choice. I continued to have a good friend there, which also was a factor that I considered when I made this decision. And if I did return to Oceanside, in a sense I'd be returning to my roots. With my friend's help, it was "Oceanside here I come." I packed up our belongings and a new life was about to unfold.

I got a job working as a "temp." Then I obtained full-time employment working for a man who was worth many millions of dollars. He was a real estate tycoon, selling land to build shopping centers, large housing developments and commercial buildings. His was one of these family-run businesses where many people were involved: wife, son, sister-in-law, nephew, as well as some friends, but throughout it all he was the man in charge. It was big business and big money as I watched, learned, and interfaced with lawyers, CPAs, accountants, and many others. There were times when I felt like I was in the TV series "Dallas" and I was watching J.R. in action. My boss was a true real estate tycoon and I was there taking it in and enjoying it all. I worked with him for ten years. He eventually closed the business for health reasons, or I'd still be there today.

In 1993, as I thought about my life, I decided to take on another pursuit, learning more about my immediate family. I had already developed an interest in genealogy, but at this time it blossomed. And a year later, in 1994, my primary focus of attention became my father. What I knew was mostly the official information that had been printed about him. There are memorials in his honor in Washington D.C., in other places in the U.S., and there is one in Korea. But the time had arrived when I wanted to get to know my father through those others who had personally interacted with him. I wanted to know all about him, everything. I contacted people from his childhood, from high school, and then from the military. It became my own personal crusade to gather as much of this information as I could, and as it progressed it was emotional and chilling.

I learned that my father was naturally protective. He was protective of his younger sister, protecting her in school, as well as at home from a mother who was abusive. And he was not one to back away from a fight, no matter who it was. The courage he displayed as a youth was the same courage that he carried with him into the Marines Corps. He was a Staff Sergeant who always put his men before himself just as he had protected his little sister; his men came first and foremost.

My desire to learn about my father helped me have a better understanding of him, of myself, of my family, and, yes, of America too. I am filled with pride that I am his daughter and hope that I, too, can continue demonstrating the kind of courage that represented the way he lived. And now, and this is because of my own personal research, when asked about this Congressional Medal of Honor recipient, I can more confidently and knowledgeably respond about this soldier, this Marine and war hero, and this man who is my father.

As I've grown older, my appetite for travel has not decreased. It had its beginnings when I lived in Germany, and during these last fifteen years I've traveled throughout much of the world. I've also been able to combine this travel with my photography. I have the fondest memories of India, South Africa, and of China and have captured my travels through my photography.

I know now, however, that Africa has become my calling and it is there where I can see wild animals in their natural habitats. Proving financial support to the endangered species as well as some of the poor villagers is an important aspect of my travel. On my first visit we were charged three times by a wild matriarch female elephant, but I was there with my cameras. This was tremendously exciting and I sold the picture of the charging elephant, along with seven or eight others, to a magazine. The charging elephant photo was placed on its front cover. I love the world and its people, but Africa is special. On my next trip I'll be there for the Great Migration with cameras ready. I can hardly wait. I've also come to believe through these travels that there is much that the United States can do to help other countries. But it is important that we address our own problems first, and then we can successfully branch out to others.

I mentioned in the beginning that I've been facing some physical setbacks. I was in a car accident in 2005 that affected my spine and as a result it was necessary for me to have spinal surgery. Then in July 2009 I fell and broke my hip. I was taken to the emergency room where the surgeon did a poor job. As a result of this poorly performed operation, and it was malpractice, I have been in a wheelchair for almost two years.

Dealing with these health issues has been challenging, but deep inside of me is the awareness about who I am and what I can accomplish. I think many of my attitudes began with my grandfather, dating back to the time when he pulled me as I rode in my sled. "You have to be tough," he said. Yes, it was grandfather who instilled this toughness in me. And then there is courage. My father exemplifies this courage and the awareness of this has helped me to deal with the various difficulties I've faced along the way.

My second hip operation was in the end of March 2010 and this time I was not taking any chances. I had two competent surgeons. Part of this recovery process includes physical therapy and I'm doing everything I need to do to resume a normal life. And I know that if I'm not walking by June 2011, I will have a full hip-replacement. It possibly should have been done more than a year earlier. I will be walking again and I know that it will be sooner, rather than later.

So that's where I am right now. When I reach my goal I will get back to my two loves: travel and photography. I will go to Africa, this time to Kenya and Tanzania for the Great Migration. My cameras will be by my side and within me will be the deepest appreciation of what it took for me to get there and what I will be seeing.

Life these past sixty-five years has been a constant journey, from early childhood to where I am today. There have been some obstacles, but I'm satisfied about how I've handled things and of what I've learned. I'm proud that I've been able to confront life head on and use those abilities that I've been given. And when I remember back to the gutsy little kid who went into the abandoned trailer, I recognize that there is still that same something deep within. I continue to be gutsy and to have that thrill of adventure. And through all of this, the "ups and the downs," the "highs and the lows," I've learned that happiness is on the inside, and cradled within me is the confidence and knowledge that when I set my mind to do something, I will succeed.

CHAPTER 5

Life's Ongoing Journey
Dick Beamer

I retired in 2003 and it's taken me some time to adjust to this new life of not working. Retirement truly was a big change from the way I had been living, but, unfortunately, I was dealing with some health issues. I had injured my back when I was young and because of that injury I was now experiencing a terrible amount of pain. People who've had back problems are aware of what I'm talking about. You're just in pain all of the time and it was so bad that at one point I even lost thirty pounds. It's taken me a long time to recover from this, but I have gotten much better. I also know that as I dealt with this, my beliefs about life, and this is directly related to my more than thirty-year involvement with AA (Alcoholics Anonymous), have given me the base for dealing with adversity and finding satisfaction, even when times have been difficult. Growing older has been a challenge.

Well, let's see. I was born in Wabash, Indiana and we were a farm family; agriculture is what is big in Indiana. Corn and soybeans are primary along with hogs. My dad died when I was two. He had high blood pressure and the doctors didn't know much about correcting it back then. He had a stroke when he was thirty-nine and was unable to work after that. He had another stroke about a year later and died. Mom then took on the responsibility of being the sole breadwinner and obtained a job in the town at a factory. I have three sisters, all of whom are older than me. Well, mom went to work in this factory and ended up marrying the boss. However, one of the differences in those years was that it was acceptable to be a heavy drinker and a heavy smoker and people didn't seem to get upset about it. My stepfather, unfortunately, was both.

We had a family picnic at the house with quite a few people over and my step-dad was doing what he normally did, drinking heavily. He'd gotten to the point where he needed to go into the house and take a nap, but as he did this he ended up falling down the stairs and severely hit his head. He was in a coma for three months and when he left the hospital he was never the same. He had to have brain surgery to relieve the pressure. He then had tremendous difficulty with language and words. He had difficulty talking and remembering. Drinking continued to be a problem and he'd become depressed.

He was not the full owner of the factory, but decided that it would be best to sell his part of it. Also, as a result of his heavy smoking he had emphysema. Phoenix was considered to be better for people with breathing problems so this became our destination. We lived in Phoenix for the next several years, but because of the heat and because of the good air quality we moved to Oceanside.

When I look back on these years I can see the result of alcoholism and the impact that it had on the family. It was a time of continued disharmony, with almost constant arguing, bickering, tension and just a general atmosphere of unhappiness. But, and this is interesting, once we made this move to Oceanside things actually got a little bit better, and I think it was because I was older and gaining my independence. I was now a junior in high school, and not only that I was sixteen and had wheels. It was an old Model "A" built in 1929, which I'd actually gotten when I was fifteen, prior to this move to Oceanside. Looking back on this now I know that it was a real rattletrap, but oh how I loved that car. It had a rumble seat where a person could sit in the back and have that complete open-air feeling. Sitting in the rumble seat also provide the occupant this temporary feeling of royalty... everyone wanted the thrill of riding in it. With my new independence, a whole new life had opened up, including dating and girls.

I made friends and went out for the football team. Football helped me to work off some of those pent up emotions. I found that on the gridiron I could excel. I know that football played a most important role at this time in my life, but I'd also fallen in love with the beach and the waves, and along came surfing. Almost immediately, after making the move from Phoenix, I'd found myself in the water and experiencing the thrill of the surf. It was really a good time.

But on the other side of the coin, unfortunately, it was also in Oceanside when I started drinking and I didn't realize its potential dangers. Even though I had personally witnessed its harmful effects in my own family, drinking was acceptable, social, and it helped me to forget that turmoil at home. I didn't know it, but in the future I would need to make some important decisions on how I wanted to live my life.

As far as those two years in high school, I don't remember that much about my teachers. There was a chemistry teacher that I liked and he taught the class well, but it was football and the team that truly stands out. We went undefeated up until CIF, and I was proud to be a part of this team. Terry Scott, the quarterback, was excellent and both offense and defense were solid. I was even written up in the paper and I still have some of those clippings. I played defense and remember scoring on two or three safeties. What an adrenalin charge! In a sense these really were the glory days. But there was something else about Oceanside and this was a real change for me. We had different races mixed together in the school and on the team: blacks, Mexicans, Samoans, Asians, and whites. I'd grown up in the land of the white man where in some places the Ku Klux Klan still played an active role. This mixing of the races truly was one of my most important lifetime experiences. I learned that friendship is deeper than the color of one's skin.

Graduation came and went, but life was getting better. After high school, I went to Mira Costa College and stayed there for two years. I was part of its very first graduating class, and then I matriculated to San Diego State. This was another significant move for me and once I'd made this I realized how happy I was to get away. My stepfather died the first year I was in San Diego. I roomed with some friends and was very fortunate. We got along well and actually helped each other to get through. I wasn't what anyone would call excessively studious or motivated and just barely got by. When the first major I had taken proved to be too demanding, I changed to a second, and then I changed to a third. I was somehow making it through, through just barely, partying too much, and as a group my friends and I were all dealing with those incredibly difficult issues of the time.

The United States was involved with Vietnam and the draft was after all of us. I knew that once I completed my degree I'd be drafted. That's the way it was in those days, and Army life, or the path of a Marine was simply not how I envisioned myself. Also, as a college student I had been exposed to the vast anti-war movement. So I made a decision and joined the Air Force, with its five-year commitment. Before going in, I took the series of tests and qualified for Officer's Training School. I went through the required training and became an officer and then became a navigator. I flew "B-52s" in Vietnam

Now, and this still seems a bit strange to me, but we flew most of our missions over South Vietnam, and we were based in Thailand. There was a kind of gentleman's agreement that if we concentrated our bombings in South Vietnam, they wouldn't shoot us down. The North Vietnamese Army had a number of SAM (Surface-to-Air Missiles) but agreed that they would only shoot us down if we flew over North Vietnam. So I spent most of my time doing bombing runs in South Vietnam and on the famous Ho Chi Ming Trail. These bombings were something that I was directly involved with, but even though I was directly involved in this, it never seemed right to me. Throughout this time, I was continually confronted with my own personal feelings and conscience about what I was directly involved with. My tour of duty ended in Vietnam and I returned to the U.S.

I was now stationed in Michigan with the Strategic Air Command, but I soon realized that for me I'd gone from the frying pan into the fire. With the Strategic Air Command, I was part of the system of defense that utilized nuclear weapons. The B 52s were carrying nuclear weapons and I would see them loaded into the bomb bay doors. What I'd been doing in Vietnam and Thailand had been difficult, but now I was dealing with nuclear weapons. I actually became sick to my stomach about having to be involved with this. Drinking became more of a problem, but I knew that in regard to my specific responsibilities in the Air Force I had to make a significant change. I applied to be a CO, a Conscientious Objector. This was a tremendous risk. I could have been put into the brig for a long time, or given the silent treatment on the job. It was necessary for many friends to substantiate my beliefs, which they did. I was immediately yanked off my assignment and given a desk job. This was the right thing for me to do and I'm proud that I was able to stand up for these beliefs. I think God was on my side.

I'm going to backtrack a little now. I met my wife when I was in navigator school in Sacramento. I was twenty-four and she was a twenty-one year old student in Sacramento State. After I served my five years in the Air Force and returned, and after we'd been married for six years, my issues with alcohol had not gone away. She was getting fed up with this, and to be honest I'd already recognized I had a problem. I know that it could have gotten a lot worse, but I joined AA and loved it right from the beginning. I knew it was right for me and because of it I nipped my drinking in the bud at a very early age.

I continue to attend these meeting around three times a week and I still benefit from them. The people are honest, caring, and willing to help others. This is the path I've chosen and I've benefited in so many ways: as a husband, as a teacher, as a father and as a person. There are twelve steps. I'm going to present them here because I believe that some of these may have significance for others as well, and you don't have to be an alcoholic to realize how important one or two of them may be to you.

The Twelve Steps:

1. We admitted we were powerless over alcohol—that our lives had become unmanageable.

2. Came to believe that a Power greater than ourselves could restore us to sanity.

3. Made a decision to turn our will and our lives over to the care of God as we understood Him.

4. Made a searching and fearless moral inventory of our selves.

5. Admitted to God, to ourselves, and to another human being the exact nature of our wrongs.

6. Were entirely ready to have God remove all these defects of character.

7. Humbly asked Him to remove our shortcomings.

8. Made a list of all persons we had harmed, and became willing to make amends to them all.

9. Made direct amends to such people wherever possible, except when to do so would injure them or others.

10. Continued to take personal inventory and when we were wrong promptly admitted it.

11. Sought through prayer and meditation to improve our conscious contact with God *as we understood Him*, praying only for knowledge of His will for us and the power to carry that out.

12. Having had a spiritual awakening as the result of these steps, we tried to carry this message to alcoholics, and to practice these principles in all our affairs.

I am fortunate. I was able to confront my problem early enough and not have it ruin my life and the lives of others. I am fortunate that my wife is very considerate, but marriage hasn't always been easy and we've had to work on it. I'm sure there were times when we both were frustrated and wanted to give up, but we didn't. We continued and our communication got better. There are times in marriage when one or the other, or both want to win. Instead of working together, you're in conflict and dealing with competition. This doesn't work, but communication does. You have to listen to the other person and understand that both of you are actually part of the problem. You have to care about the relationship and making it work, rather than trying to win or prove that you're right.

My wife saw what I was going through when I joined AA and she joined Al-Anon, for friends and families of alcoholics. She's gone beyond this and has become involved with her church. It began with her working with the youth, but she's gone into the seminary and now is an itinerant minister, filling in when a church needs someone. She continues to take classes in the seminary. I have a good marriage and my wife is a very good person.

After I got out of the service, we moved to Wabash, Indiana where I was born. We saw this beautiful little farm and bought it in 1972. We paid thirty-one thousand for forty-six acres and it's probably worth ten to fifteen times that amount now. I first worked as a social worker, but went back to school and completed my requirements to become a teacher. It took about a year and a half to complete and this second time around was quite an exhilarating experience. I was motivated, interested, and focused on learning. I was totally involved in the educational process and not just doing the minimal to get by. I am proud of what I was able to accomplish and obtained my teaching credential.

My hobby is flying, which is a natural follow up from my time in the Air Force, and I've had a dozen different planes over the years. Now I have an antique open cockpit plane, but I've had ultra lights. I've actually had to crash land several times, which sounds very dangerous, but in an ultra light this is very easy. You just coast back down.

I taught the fifth grade for twenty-five years and retired in 2003, and I credit my involvement with AA for helping me to become a better teacher. I think one of the highlights of my career occurred in 2000. I was able to obtain a grant and special permission to fly myself out to California and document the entire journey. We had a webpage set up and used the information for all of the various classes taught at the school. Actually, it was totally unprecedented and we ended up doing this same thing three years in a row. Eventually I did this with rivers and the kids put me in a canoe with a laptop, water testing equipment, a tent, sleeping bag, food, and my bicycle. I emailed them the different readings of water pollution. I paddled 450 miles down the Wabash, to the Mississippi, spending seven weeks on the trip. I would sleep on islands, reminiscent of the adventures of Tom Sawyer. The islands were pristine and the water was much healthier than we anticipated. This truly was a wonderful experience.

I know as I taught these many years that because of my own family background and the difficulties that I'd experienced, I had a better understanding of the kinds of things some kids go through. I loved teaching and loved science and that made it easy. Kids think science is fun, but it was quite emotionally exhausting and would wear me down. There is a constant stress that takes its toll. The parents, however, were extremely supportive and we would have 95% of the parents show up for the back-to-school programs. However, because of the back problems, it was time to give it up.

As I grow older I know that I'm still learning. We always have challenges to face, but this causes us to grow. It's not always easy and it can be painful, but it's the way it happens and the way life is. I lost thirty pounds because of my back and became very discouraged but I kept going, and my back is now much better. I go to my meetings, teach at the junior college and I try to focus on how I can serve others. The important thing is to continue to accept the challenges you face.

I am now a grandpa. I'm Grandpa Beamer and that is important to me. My own grandfather, the original Grandpa Beamer, was a great role model and I'm enjoying this. For now, however, I simply want to continue to stumble my way forward, and, hopefully, continue to serve others and to do what I believe is God's will.

CHAPTER 6

One Day at a Time
Gary Wilkins (GW)

Let's get down to the basics. I no longer go by the name Gary. Simply call me "GW" and as we get started with this I need to let you know that I'm dealing with cancer. I got diagnosed with prostate cancer about a year and a half ago. I'll talk about this and how it's affects me as we go along. But for me, these past fifty years have been a heck of a ride; I've done a lot and learned a lot. Oceanside, and this isn't to disparage the school in any way, doesn't bring back a whole lot of memories. I think it's actually a part of my life that I'd rather forget, but here goes. I began there at the start of the ninth grade. My dad was a carpet and tile layer in San Diego and he got a job in Oceanside in 1959. I was all of fourteen years old, but let's just put it like this: I was fourteen with an attitude. Everyone's heard of the difficult teenage years, well that was me with about three exclamation points. I had no respect for authority and made sure everyone knew it. I was what I would call "a nasty little fart."

But there was one teacher that I liked and that was Mr. Simcox. I respected him and will always remember him. In both high school and college he had been a football player and he had been very good. He was a coach for the Oceanside football team, which I was a part of for awhile, and also one of my teachers. He didn't get upset like the other teachers and coaches when people did something wrong, and he respected all of the players. His manner was calm, but you knew he was in control. I was a challenge to all of my teachers and maybe even to him sometimes, but I held him then and now in the deepest respect. The football stadium at Oceanside was named after him and he died of cancer. It seems kind of strange and in a way comforting that I will follow him down the same path. Cancer will have gotten each of us.

Oceanside High School had a Bible Club back then and I belonged to it. At one time I was even the president but that was not to last. I remember there was one Mexican girl who'd come to it, but not many others. It wasn't right for me at that time and I quit.

There was a teacher who was gay, though that was not a term that we used back then. He wasn't my teacher, but it still bothered me the way he was. We also had a student who was gay. I was a macho young teenager and society was much harder on gays back then. I believed that this type of sexual orientation was wrong back then and I still believe it is wrong, but I've also come to realize that there is nothing that I can do about it.

Here's something that I remember. In P.E, when the fields were soaked after a heavy rainstorm, the teachers would have us play a game called "Scrunch." Basically this was a free-for-all and the teachers threw out a ball and let us just run back and forth and pound on each other. I got into a fight during this game of scrunch and got suspended. Fighting was an automatic suspension.

I was rebellious and difficult, and throughout these years I didn't feel that my parents were very supportive. But I also know that I gave them many difficult moments. I lasted until my senior year and then I got kicked out of both school and home. After this, I was no longer living at home and I was doing a variety of jobs. This was the way it was for two years, but at that time in our country war was going on. Vietnam was really heating up and many of my friends were being drafted. I knew that I didn't want to go into the Army or the Marines, and many people who were drafted found themselves in the Marines, so in April of 1965, I did the unthinkable. I joined the Air Force. Vietnam was going on strong and in the service you have to do what you're told and take orders. I was rebellious, defiant, and had more than a few issues with authority figures. It was a hard go...but in some ways it turned out to be good. I hadn't graduated from high school and through the service I got my GED. But I also have to thank them for the training they provided. I was trained as a heavy-duty equipment operator and I became proficient with all the different types of heavy-duty equipment. I definitely was not the service type, but in some ways I consider myself lucky. I got some good training, passed the GED, and I didn't have to go to Vietnam.

Three years, six months and twenty-four days later I was finally released and could leave. I knew exactly how many days I'd served. I'd counted each day and this getting out was an event. It was also incredible the way that it happened. It was called an "early out." President Johnson, bless his heart, let a whole bunch of us leave before serving the full amount of time and I got released six months early. I was out and this training they provided proved to be quite useful. I became a heavy equipment operator in California. Country music was also becoming popular at the time and I was especially good at the Texas Two-Step. I was so good, in fact, that from 1975 to 1979, I used to teach it.

During the seventies, I was driving heavy equipment and I loved it: bulldozers, scrapers, and some of the other equipment. Believe it when I tell you this that it is a creative work and one where you can see the progress. You're the one that handles this large equipment and it takes skill. Yes, this was a challenge and I loved it, but people found out I could do surveying. Because of this ability they took me off the equipment. I was called a "grade checker" and was in charge of telling others what to do. The excitement and the fun of the job were taken out. In 1980, I retired and went onto other challenges. I've been quite fortunate to have things go the way they have.

I ended up moving to Texas where I changed careers and became a deputy sheriff. At one time I was going nowhere and now I realize that I've enjoyed the kind of success that I'd only dreamed of. To become a deputy sheriff it took 500 hundred hours of training. There was a lot of physical conditioning that included running, jumping and even some swimming and I did it all. I was determined to get myself through. I learned everything that an officer needs to learn. I also became an NRA shooting instructor.

I worked in Houston where we have many gangs and serious offenders. I spent some time working in the jail and we had some of the worst of the worst there: killers, child molesters, and gang members from all the different gangs. One of the worst gangs is called "MS 13" and they're from El Salvador. They don't care who you are. They will shoot you and they're all very, very bad. We have both Hispanic and black gangs and one thing that I've seen is that they don't get along. In fact, most of the gangs don't get along with each other.

Later, after working in the jail, I was assigned to the courts and became a bailiff. This was not the same kind of stress, but there were times when we'd have fights right in court. People didn't like their sentences or something else and they would start to fight. Then the sheriffs would be called into break it up. I have a few scars from some of these fights, but in every case I can say with pride that we handled the problems.

One of the issues the city was dealing with was that they simply didn't want to admit that they had gangs. It's a political thing and it's bad to say that these problems exist. Well, what we saw was that denial of problems doesn't work. The gangs are there and they just aren't going to go away and this isn't just in Houston, but in many other cities also. And Mexico—just look at Mexico—many thousands of people have been killed down there and the government has no control. In Mexico the cartels run the show. But, fortunately, that's not the case here and in Houston they've learned they have to deal with this problem.

Over the years, I'd been married and divorced three times and I know that for much of this time I must have been hard to live with. Drinking was an issue that had taken a toll on my family and me, and on top of this I was also a smoker. Twenty-five years ago I met the woman of my life and I fell deeply, madly in love. She's ten years older than me and when she was a young girl she had polio. I knew that if I were going to stay with her and have this marriage be a success I would have to change. I knew that I couldn't be the person she needed, if I continued in my old ways so I changed. In one day I gave up drinking and smoking and I haven't had a drink or a cigarette in the past twenty-five years...actually I did once but gagged.

My wife and I have a wonderful relationship and have done some truly amazing things. For ten years we'd go on the motorcycle and travel places. I have a three-wheeler motorcycle. She has a wheelchair and we'd take it with us. There's even a little ramp that we'd take and I'd push her up the ramp. Then I'd pick her up and put her on the motorcycle and off we'd go again. We traveled through much of the United States: Washington, the northern states, then to Florida and Virginia. Every time we had a vacation we'd go someplace and this was a time that the two of us cherish dearly.

I retired from the police department in 2008 and as I said in the beginning I've got cancer. My wife is confined to a wheelchair and I want to be there to help her as much as I can, but my doctors tell me not to do too much. What I have is a slow type of cancer and it went from my prostate to my bones. Since then it has metastasized to my liver and lungs. My doctors told me in September that I had anywhere from six months to a year to live and its now been six months. I have a pump that injects me with painkillers and I take eight different pills every day to kill the pain. I'm having more difficulty walking, but my focus remains on God.

I go to church as much as I am able and I live my life for God. I've turned everything over to the Lord. Whatever He wants, that's the way it's going to be and I can't feel sorry for myself. I know I'm going through a lot, but I don't want to make others suffer simply because I hurt. I leave it to the Lord. I'm going to continue my life living for Him and I love the Lord. God is the way and God has protected me throughout my life. If you put everything you have into worshiping God and Jesus Christ, your problems will go away. Jesus died on the cross for us. If you really believe deep in your heart and you take Jesus Christ as your personal savior you won't have any problems. If you give them to Him you won't have any problems and I don't have problems. People at church tell me I look fine. They say I look healthy, but I know I should be home in bed. I know what's going on with me. If He wants me tonight that's His choice. His will is what will happen. The Lord is in charge and the Lord knows it is my wish to continue to take care of my wife. I take it day by day and do whatever I can, but the Lord is with me. I'm happy, extremely happy.

(GW passed away on April 19, 2010 at 12:47 A.M)

CHAPTER 7

The Art of Happiness
Janey Quigley Anderson

As much as I like to think of my life as normal and simple, my birth was anything but normal, and definitely not simple. I was born six weeks premature with *erthroblastosis fetalis*, a condition from which few children survived at that time. I was an Rh-positive baby with an Rh-negative mother, and I was the third child in the family. When this happens, usually occurring after the second or third birth, the mother's antibodies gang up on the unborn fetus. I was in fact the third baby in the world to survive with this condition that year. The doctors told my parents that there was no way that I would live, but, fortunately, we had a pediatrician who had read various medical journals concerning this condition and what could be done. Immediately after I was born a complete blood transfusion was performed and it was because of this I am here today. I was totally cured and I know that I am most fortunate. I believe the very fact that I survived has helped me to be grateful for my life and all of those things that I have experienced.

My dad was in communications for a television station in Missouri. When I was young, unfortunately, I suffered from a variety of allergies and because of this my parents decided to move to California and to Oceanside. They believed the climate would be better for me.

I was four when I entered South Oceanside Elementary School, but I still had to deal with health issues. I missed half of kindergarten and the first grade because of rheumatic fever, the effects of which would come back to create difficulties for me. Later as I progressed through both elementary and junior high school, I was the youngest in my class.

My memories of these early years, and this includes both my elementary and junior high school experiences, were happy and fun-filled with many friends and with teachers who I believed to be excellent. In fact, I stayed in contact with my sixth grade teacher, Mrs. Shaw, and my third grade teacher, Mrs. Barlow.

High school, however, was a different story and I believe this was the case not just for me, but also for many others. There seemed to be a kind of aloofness and rigidity in the way most of the teachers ran their classes, possibly a reflection of the educational philosophy of that time, as well as reflecting within these teachers what I consider to be a general lack of feeling or compassion for the students. Students were categorized by their counselors and then pigeonholed into classes, and a predetermined type of academic expectation was created. Certainly it wasn't this way in all cases, but this seemed to be the dominant way of thinking at that time. But there were other things more disturbing than just the way teachers and counselors categorized you and the way they gave out their grades. Some of the teachers' attitudes were quite disheartening. I know from my years as a teacher the importance of having a positive attitude and the value of acknowledging each student's self worth: each and every student is very special with their own special gifts.

Here's an example of a teacher at Oceanside High with an attitude that I'll never forget. Because of my early difficulties with rheumatic fever my family doctor, Dr. Harvey, recommended that I take only two years of physical education. At this time four years of physical education were required for graduation. My junior year I had a great teacher and did not experience any problems with her regarding my inability to participate, but my senior year I ran into a brick wall. This teacher disliked me for being excused from participation and was determined to take her dislike (anger, resentment) out on me.

Now keep in mind I had not wanted my situation to be this way. I wanted to play sports like everyone else and I loved physical activity, but I was following my doctor's orders. This teacher had a very bad attitude and told me daily I had to pick up the dirty towels. Then towards the end of the school year we had "Senior Dress Up Day." I came to school dressed appropriately for this special day and she demanded that I not just clean the dirty equipment, but the entire equipment room. This to me was clearly an inappropriate demand on her part as well as placing me in an awkward position. I wasn't suitably dressed for what she was demanding and I refused. I was sent to Mrs. Morse, the Girls Vice Principal. I told Mrs. Morse what had happened and that this "demand" was inappropriate, especially considering the way I was dressed and that I wouldn't do it. I respected Mrs. Morse and she told me that I had to do it and I returned to the gym and I tried. But as I attempted to do what was requested of me I knew that this would ruin my dress. I didn't do it and the teacher then gave me an "F."

I will never forget how this teacher treated me, but it was through this experience I began to learn what has become part of my philosophy on life: "When you're given a lemon, make lemonade."

After high school I was determined to go straight to college, even though this was not the recommendation from my counselors. Remember this was at a time when students were pigeonholed by their teachers and counselors. My counselor, in fact, had stated to me on several occasions that going off to college was not a good decision and that the best I should hope for would be to go to the junior college. Well, I didn't heed her advice and to this day I'm glad that I didn't. I was sure I could be successful in college and I got into college by taking the challenge test. I did well enough and was accepted to the original Pepperdine University located in Watts. It was a wonderful school with good teachers and the overall environment was excellent. And even though it was located in Watts, it was very safe, but after spending two years there I knew I wanted a change.

Pepperdine is a Church of Christ school and the education was excellent, but I knew that if I wanted to have a truly broad education and be exposed more directly to those critical issues which our society was dealing, I needed to make a change; and after two years at Pepperdine I had proven to myself that I could be successful. This awareness and self-confidence helped provide the necessary impetus for such a change.

I transferred to Fresno State and graduated, later completing a life teaching credential at Chapman College. Immediately after my graduation from Fresno State, and it was only ten days later on February 10, 1969, I went right into the teaching profession as a fifth grade teacher. I did not have a credential and had not completed any student teaching or taken any teacher preparatory classes. I was teaching on a Provisional Teaching Credential. It was either "sink or swim." My survival depended on getting the lessons done, handling student discipline and parent conferences, completing the required testing, and all the time attending classes at night to finish the required teaching credential.

I quickly learned a teacher teaches students, not just subjects. Meeting the needs of each student is a prime ingredient for obtaining student success and teacher effectiveness. In June of 1974, I received my teaching credential.

I was married February 1, 1969. My husband and I wanted to become parents but were informed by various doctors that we could not have children. Both of us very much wanted to be parents so we adopted. Then after this adoption, "boom," and this is frequently the kind of thing that happens, I became pregnant, and then I became pregnant again. From having no kids, suddenly we had three and it took me ten years to get back to teaching full time.

In teaching, frequently I have had to deal with children who have special needs. My adopted son Nick has been a special needs child and is neurologically handicapped. Because of my experiences with him and with similar types of students within my classroom, I have learned a lot about helping children with special needs, and I've personally learned just how difficult it can be to deal with a rigid educational system. My son was diagnosed with fine-motor impairment and dyscalculia (excessive difficulties with math, numbers are reversed), ADHD (Attention Deficit Disorder with Hyperactivity) and gross social immaturity. Intelligence testing (this was completed three times) indicated that he fell within the superior to the gifted range of intelligence.

As part of the process of obtaining help for him I took him to the Neurological-Psychological Development Center in San Diego for a complete evaluation. I knew we needed to have a thorough evaluation of him done. I ran into various roadblocks and resistance within his school system to provide adequately for his needs, so I wrote to the state and obtained support from the California Department of Education. They sent a mediator to look over the assessment results and check to see what steps the district had taken in providing the appropriate setting and placement. The mediator then made a final recommendation. He determined that the district where my son attended school had not met its obligations and because of this we were able to send our son to a special (California Certified) school in Terrero, New Mexico. It was excellent. The name of the school was "Brush Ranch." Not long after Nick was at Brush Ranch, the California State Department of Education sent out a consultant from UCLA to look further into the county's failure to meet their special education obligations. She, too, found the county schools to be in what is termed "Non-Compliance."

Brush Ranch's philosophy and approach to teaching provided the ideal setting for him to progress. They held a deep respect for all the children and they had a small teacher-student ratio. They taught each child learning strategies that would enable them to progress to their abilities and they provided counselors to deal with the social and emotional concomitants that go hand in hand with learning disabilities. Learning deficits are a common occurrence and can occur within any family, and at this school we were able to see how many families are affected. Sylvester Stallone, James Brolin, and Eileen Brennan all had sons who were there. A child from one of the justices in the Supreme Court in Texas was there, as well as various ambassadors' kids, and quite a few other well-known personalities had children there. In fact, kids from all over the world attended. They flew the flags of 48 different countries from which children had matriculated. My son, and I am most proud of this, received "Writer of the Year" award from Random House Publishing at the 1990 Brush Ranch Commencement. This was an amazing accomplishment for Nick considering his deficits were extreme in the written language areas. Later he went on to junior college and then he joined the Air Force. He is now out of the Air Force and working in the private sector, but the value of this earlier education and the assistance he received while at Brush Ranch I believe is responsible for much of the success he is now having.

What I went through in obtaining help for him provided me with a tremendous learning experience, and from this school in New Mexico I could directly see how the appropriate education can positively impact not just a special needs child, but all children. This school's indirect influence on me, which I learned through their interventions with my son, helped to reinforce the knowledge that a teacher can make a big difference in the lives of his or her students. And through my direct experiences, as both a parent and teacher, I became knowledgeable about how to deal with and help these special needs' children. Marysville Unified, where I worked, let me teach in-service classes on how to teach attention deficit disorder kids. As a teacher it is important to know how to teach those who learn differently. It has been my experience that many teachers don't know how to deal with special needs students, but frequently the colleges don't teach or prepare new teachers on how to deal with children who have special needs, and those who learn differently. One of the biggest downfalls in dealing with a special needs' child is that many teachers forget how important it is to "respect" each and every one of these students, providing the same respect to them as you would to all the students.

Marysville is one of the poorest areas within the state and unemployment currently runs at about twenty-two percent. We have many homeless kids. I loved working there and I loved the students. Many of my students came from the central and coastal parts of Mexico and many of their parents had been educated in Mexico. Some of these parents were professionals. Most of my Hispanic parents were gainfully employed. But we didn't just have students from Mexico, they came from other countries and we had quite a few from Laos. I hold a Language Development Specialist Certificate and taught each year with a minimum of six different languages in my classes.

I loved my years of teaching and working with students, but there were also times when it was heart wrenching; some of these students faced such tremendous difficulties. Age and exhaustion set in and I knew I needed to say goodbye. It was time to retire. I am proud of what I have accomplished and I will carry these memories with me forever.

My other two children have graduated from college and both are married and parents themselves. All three are different with his or her distinct personality and each has taught me so much. I've also seen how they are confronted with issues with which my husband and I did not have to deal. My daughter is a teacher and her husband has a degree in engineering, and worked in the biotech field. Because of the economic situation he has lost his job. She is now the sole provider as he looks for a new job. In some ways the world and the economic conditions seem to be much more difficult than when my husband and I were young, working, and starting our family.

Over the years, I have gained a tremendous respect for the Salvation Army and how they have helped the poorer families in the community. They provide food, clothing and often shelter for these families. My husband and I give as much support to this organization as we are able.

When I look back on my life and what I think is important, there are several things that stand out. The first is what my mother used to say: "When you're honest with yourself, you will be honest with other people." I think many people try to fool themselves and do something that is in conflict with their values and with what they really need to be happy.

I also believe that one of the secrets to happiness is to look at things that happen to us, no matter what they are, and see that there is also something positive that results. When bad things happen it's important to stop and count your blessings. Like everyone I've had a few bumps in the road of life, but these made me stronger and also gave me a sense of compassion for what others go through. I'm a very grateful person and I'm a very happy person. Often it's the simple things that make for the most happiness. For me, my husband and children are the greatest blessing.

I've been married for forty-two years. Marriage is something that you work on together. You want the best for the other person and each of you give one hundred percent. It means your commitment is there and you're working not as two, but as one. Yes, I've been a happy camper for many years.

And lastly and most importantly within my life I have a connection with God. I know that I can pray and that my prayers will be answered. Maybe not in the way I thought, but it always turns out for the best. I feel a very close connection and know that God is there all the time. God is love and is not here to punish us or to have us live in fear, but to simply provide His support and love. In many ways my life is simple... and that's the way it needs to be.

I retired from the Mary Covillaud School in June 2009. This is one of the oldest schools in California at 152 years. Even though I am retired I still believe in helping. I have been a volunteer advocate for special education students at their IEP meetings. This is something that I believe in. For years I was a master teacher working with both Sacramento State University and Chico State University, taking many of their student teachers under my wings and into my classroom.

Life is a learning experience, but happiness I know is not based on the external, but rather comes from the inside. I almost didn't survive when I was born, but I'm still here and seeing each day as a blessing. Make the most of each day.

CHAPTER 8

The Art of Living
Thomas Stettler

It takes a long time to find out who you really are and determine your priorities and the manner in which you choose to live. In some ways I've gone through the school of hard knocks, but this is also how I've learned. I've also come to recognize that I'm not like many of the others with whom I graduated, and with the passing of time I'm even more aware of my individuality; but I'm proud of who I've become. I'm comfortable with where I am in my life and with myself, which is most important, and I realize that I've been able to adjust to a wide variety of circumstances and through it all to live it my way. Oh, and I've retained my sense of humor and been able to see life as an experience that is meant to be enjoyed.

Let's begin with my family's history in Oceanside because it goes back a long time. In fact, during the turn of the twentieth century my great-grandfather was a gun-toting marshal who rode the county on horseback. He covered many parts of Oceanside and the San Luis Rey Valley. Most of the people at this time were farmers and for them it was quite an excursion to go to the beaches, and it was because of this that Oceanside got its name. These farmers stated it this way: "We're going to the ocean side." Eventually it simply became Oceanside.

And as far as my great grandfather is concerned, I don't really know much about him except that I've inherited his badge. Every now and then I look at it and it reads: "Deputy City Marshall, Oceanside, California."

After my great grandfather, there was my grandfather, Joseph M. Trotter, Sr., and he graduated from the original Oceanside High School in 1920, a high school with a total of nine students in his graduating class. It was around this time when Oceanside High School actually had just come into existence. The main building was constructed in 1906. Joseph M. Trotter, Sr. had a son, Joseph M. Trotter, Jr., and at one time he was the principal at Jefferson Junior High School. My uncle was teaching at Jefferson when I attended there from 1956 to 1958.

My mom is still alive and doing fairly well. She's eighty-seven. I consider her to be the resident historian of Oceanside, remembering how it used to be. She can tell you many stories about various events, where specific people used to live, and how the city has changed since its earlier days. She is one of the few remaining residents whose entire life has been exclusively in this city and who continues to be an "Oceansider," through and through. Mom also graduated from Oceanside High in the class of 1941. They will be having their seventieth high school reunion coming up in another year and her brother graduated in the 1939 class. He died several years ago.

Here's something interesting: at Oceanside we all know that Camp Pendleton is an integral part of the community, but it wasn't so for my mom. The area where Camp Pendleton is located was originally known as the "Rancho Santa Margarita y las Flores" and it was part of a Spanish land grant comprising more than one hundred twenty-two thousand acres. It was only when World War II broke out that Camp Pendleton came into existence. It's considered to be the largest Marine Corps training area in the nation. They've also made many war movies there, with the beaches providing the perfect setting for many amphibious assaults.

When I was young, Oceanside was small in comparison to what it is now. In fact, if I remember correctly, the total population up until 1956 was less than fifteen thousand. (Now its population is approaching two hundred thousand.) At first we lived in South Oceanside and my dad was a plastering contractor, priding himself on building the various houses that we lived in. He had developed his own system. We'd live in a house for several years and then he'd sell it for twice what it cost him to make, and he'd do it again. Build a house, live in it, and sell it for more money. In some ways he was the original entrepreneur, an idea that later was taken to the extreme several years ago with the concept of "flipping" houses.

I attended South Oceanside Elementary School until the sixth grade. Then because of over-crowding–the baby boom was affecting the schools–my sixth grade class was put on a school bus and transported to Laurel Street Elementary School. We were the white, middle class kids being bused into a minority area comprised primarily of Hispanics and African-Americans. This busing started in September of 1955, well before desegregation was to be issue in the U.S., and long before any of us were to realize that this entire event could have been even the slightest bit controversial. For the first couple of days or even weeks, it was somewhat strained as the various ethnic groups adjusted to each other, but when things settled down something magical happened. We all got along. I made new friends who would remain so all the way through high school. But, and this is important when understanding the differences between over fifty years ago and now...we didn't have gangs. We could just be ourselves and be friends.

After Laurel Street School, I attended Jefferson Junior High School where I had Mrs. Freeberg in the seventh grade, possibly the best teacher I've ever had. She would read to us a variety of stories from Edgar Allen Poe and other authors and she'd actually memorized some of their entire works. She would recite these poems, stories and so on without the use of a book or notes. She kept the entire class in complete suspense and awe as we listened to the stories, always impressed that she was able to do this, and we all knew that she had a deep love of teaching and the students.

But junior high school was much more than the academics and simply listening to stories. Something strange was going on within me and I began to be somewhat distracted. Girls had come onto the scene and I was one of the more courageous of the typically shy junior high school male. I had gone through basic dance training known as cotillion, which my parents had insisted upon. So, not only did I faithfully attend these dances, but I also danced with the girls. When I look back on this I recognize my life was destined to never again be the same. And then came love, only to feel the crush of rejection. My heart was broken, but, fortunately, not beyond repair and I made a speedy recovery. Girls were not just on the horizon, but they were in my classes. I had my first kiss, an unforgettable moment that will live with me forever.

Junior high school lasted for two years with high school being next. My ninth grade year began at Carlsbad High School. My sister was going there and had encouraged me to attend, but Carlsbad wasn't for me. My best friends were in Oceanside and after just one year in Carlsbad I knew that Oceanside was where I wanted to be. I wanted to be a Pirate and in my sophomore year I made the switch. Oceanside High School had become my home.

One thing I must emphasize is that I was not what anyone would consider as an exemplary student. I got by, sometimes just barely, and as the saying goes, "by the skin of my teeth," but on the more positive side I got along with my fellow classmates quite well. When I did graduate my overall GPA was something pretty close to a 2.0, so you can see that I was not one of those who was deemed most likely to succeed in college by my counselors, but all was well. I had friends, parties, and girls on my mind. Life was good.

In 1961, my persona took on a newer and more vibrant look. My great aunt gave me my first car, a 1949 Ford. I also got my driver's license on my sixteenth birthday, which was also in 1961. I was, using the term of the day, "stoked." But, as bad luck would have it, after about a year my car was "totaled." I got rear-ended and my dream car was no more. It was junked, except for the engine. It was at this moment when I became aware of just how important my good friend, Gary Borden, the expert mechanic of the class of 1963, really was. In one weekend we took the engine out of the ex-dream machine and placed it in a 1951 Woody. I was back in business and in sole possession of one of the most famous autos of that time period. "Woodys" hardly exist nowadays and they're worth a fortune. It was my favorite car of all time.

Like most students I attended football and basketball games. Typically we'd have a pep rally before a big game, holding it in the gym to build up enthusiasm. We'd have these yelling contests between the different classes to see who was the most raucous and the seniors almost always won. Then, whether it was football or basketball, we'd go to those Friday night games. They were always fun, but there were two basketball games against Vista High School, which to this very day I rate as the best of all time. Vista had become our archenemy and the games were always tightly fought; up until the very last minute there was no way to know who would win. Both my junior and senior years, and I'm not sure how it started, the games exploded, like a canister of dynamite going off as players and spectators flooded onto the court in a grand display of adolescent pugilism. It was complete chaos with fights everywhere. One minute it was a basketball game and the next it was a hundred people going at it. Mike Lyons, a member of our class, who later became a professional golfer, after watching the action felt that he, too, wanted to get involved. He went onto the floor and immediately got punched in the face. "I just got punched in the face," he said as he returned to the bleachers and sat down. We then resumed watching all of the action.

There was Tula Solita, one of the most memorable members of our class. Tula was bigger than the rest of us and quite strong. In fact, his father was the king of Samoa who was serving in the Marine Corps. In Oceanside, all of the Samoans lived in this large house several blocks from the pier; I think at least twenty or thirty Samoans lived there. I can remember driving by and Tula's father would be sitting in front of the house in all of his regalia, Samoan style. And Tula was not someone to be messed with. Once this other student challenged him to a fight and Tula responded, out of fear of being kicked out, "No, I don't want to fight." He'd been in several other fights and he even backed away, but this boy wouldn't take no for an answer. He kicked Tula hard in the gonads. Tula proceeded to beat the crap out of him. When it was over Tula turned to me and said: "Ya know that really hurt what he did." I couldn't believe it. If that had happened to me, I would have been flattened.

My memories of most of the classes are minimal, except for P.E. and Coach Wagner. At this time corporal punishment was alive and well, and Coach Wagner gave out what were known as "spots." For doing something wrong or not dressing for P.E., he would say, "You just got a "spot-a-roonie." In order to remove them and raise your grade you could take a swat. "Bend over and touch your toes," he'd say, and then "bang!" I once had three swats and I've got to tell you they hurt like hell. Oh, and I was on the wrestling team. I owned the only pair of wrestling shoes and everyone on the team borrowed them.

After high school, it was time to work. My first job was with San Diego Gas and Electric as a ditch digger. It was hard work, but at $6.75 an hour I was doing far better than the average worker who was earning about $1.25 an hour. Then I became a cook at Sambo's Restaurant. Sambo's was later to make the headlines for being racist, but it was a fun place and I had all the food I could eat. I also made an attempt at Oceanside Junior College, a feeble one at that and decided that it wasn't for me. For the time, I'd had about all I wanted to do with school.

After Sambo's, I worked at Swan Electronics where I was a metal plater. Several friends also worked there and it's always nice to work with people you know. However, the Vietnam War was getting bigger with each passing day. The newspapers and TV carried the latest reports everyday—the infamous body counts of the number of Viet Cong dead compared to our dead. Just about all boys and young men from the age of eighteen to twenty-eight were facing the prospects of military service. The Army was a-knocking and I was about to be drafted.

Now I had never considered myself the military type, at least not the Army "gung-ho" type. So when the Army sent me my notice to report, I was way ahead of them. Gary Borden and I—remember Gary who was the expert car mechanic—had taken matters into our own hands and joined the Navy on what was known as the buddy system. Gary, like me, didn't consider himself the Army type either and we went through boot camp together at the age of twenty-one. The concept in boot camp is to take civilians and change them into functioning military personnel and after experiencing it I can tell you that it works. Boot camp definitely wasn't something to be classified into the "fun and games" category, but it accomplished what it was supposed to accomplish. We were changed into functioning military personnel. Gary and I remain friends today.

After basic training, my advanced training was in fundamental electricity and electronics, and later I was sent to sonar school. This training was very good and I was a sonar technician for twelve years, working on a destroyer. "Join the Navy and see the world," and that's exactly what happened. Our deployment on ship was for a year at time, with the longest period at sea without stopping in at a port being seventy-two days. Once we were off the coast of Vietnam and were doing what was termed shore bombardment, during the Tet Offensive. Each bullet weighted fifty-four pounds. I remember we fired something like seven thousand rounds. Our guns were five inches and we had a successful hit on a North Vietnamese convoy. Several times we were fired upon from the shore, but we were never hit.

I made E-6 after four and one-half years and for the remainder of my twelve years made no further advancement. Once Vietnam had ended and we were we were no longer at war, advancement came to a standstill. During my twelve years in the Navy, I went to Vietnam three times, Japan, Hong Kong, Sri Lanka, Thailand, the Philippines, and several other places. I also was accepted into officer's candidate school and was sent to the University of New Mexico to get a degree. I would have stayed in the Navy had this worked out, but it was not to be. The problem was that I did not have the necessary math background to handle the required courses.

Though I wasn't able to complete my education at the University of New Mexico or become an officer, I realized how important it was for me to have more training in the area of math. It had been a psychological barrier and one that would raise its head in the future. The time would again come for me to test the waters and see if I could be successful.

However, before getting to my future encounters with math, I need to discuss marriage. Marriage has been a bit of a challenge for me and something I've learned through the school of hard knocks is that it doesn't suit me well. I've been married twice. There were those times in the past when I blamed this lack of matrimonial success on the other person, but I no longer think this way. I've realized that it takes two to make a marriage and that it's necessary that both people are committed and willing to work on it together.

I was twenty-three for the first marriage and it lasted about a year-and-a-half. We both knew that it wasn't going to work out and we decided to end it. With my second marriage, I was twenty-seven and it lasted for ten years. We had a daughter and I believe she is the one good thing that resulted. I'm very proud of her and believe that she has become a confident, independent and successful woman. At the age of eleven she came to live with me temporarily. But when the time came for her to go back with her mother, she decided to stay with me instead.

Life, I've learned, brings us a variety of challenges and this was to be one of the biggest for me. Suddenly, I had become a single father with a pre-adolescent daughter, and I found I enjoyed taking on the role of a single parent. Through these experiences I saw that many parents are too uptight and controlling, and that gets in the way of their relationship with their children. I wasn't an over controlling parent, allowing my daughter to have as much freedom as both she and I were comfortable with, and it worked out well. Most of her friends preferred hanging out at our house and I also enjoyed this.

It helped that she was quite bright, a gifted student, and graduated from high school with honors. The credit I take is that I let her be herself and to develop in the way that was most natural for her. She's now graduated from the University of Maryland in chemistry and is working in research. I'm proud of her and can see that she's become her own person, and we continue to have a close relationship. And over the years I've been able to keep good communication with her mother, and that is the way as it should be. Yes, the two of us have gone our own individual ways and she's remarried, but we aren't angry with each. We've just gone down separate paths.

I was thirty-three when I decided to leave the Navy and go back to junior college. I was ready to dedicate myself to academics. I earned my AA Degree in Electronics with a GPA of 3.8. Older and wiser I believe holds true for me here and everything that I'd experienced since high school had been good for me. I was no longer the same person who had lacked motivation and self-confidence in the past. Math had been my psychological Achilles heel, my primary area of frustration, and I decided to attack it head on. I began with basic algebra and worked my way up. I continued with math until I'd taken Calculus, and I did well. I obtained a job as a technical writer and illustrator for engineers. I have now changed professions and am a Share Point administrator, Third Marine Air Wing. This has been both challenging and exciting and I've been able to utilize the knowledge I have gained over the years.

So that hits the major areas of my life. I still work and I live by myself in San Diego. I have a cat. I believe it's important to have friends and I maintain friendships from the past. In spite of two marriages that didn't work out, I still enjoy and love women. And what has been even more important, I find that they enjoy and love me, but getting involved in another marriage, well...

Happiness, and this is no matter where you are or what is happening in your life, is on the inside. I've also learned that you have to love yourself and as we go through this aging process, this most important. You're not perfect. So what!

And it's vital to have a sense of humor. Laugh, enjoy, and just take it one day at a time. No matter what is going on, don't let that particular thing or unfortunate event prevent you from enjoying each moment. Eventually that problem or issue will be resolved and you'll come to a solution, but learn as you go along. Don't blame others. Learn from your experiences and from what life is teaching you.

And take my advice, live in the present, enjoy each and every moment, and be sure to laugh. And when you can do this, you will know with confidence that whatever it is that the future has to bring, it will be good.

CHAPTER 9

A Helping Hand
Robin Prestwood

I was one of those Marine brats so common in Oceanside, and because of my father's military obligations I had moved to various schools all of my life. When I entered Oceanside I was to begin at Jefferson Junior High School. Prior to this, I'd already changed schools something like six times. I grew up with the feeling that just when I was getting settled and making friends, it was time to pack up and move again. I didn't like it when this happened, but in retrospect I don't view these moves negatively. They taught me to adjust to unfamiliar environments and to a different set of circumstances. With each move, I would have to make new friends and again prove myself with my teachers. Those moves were to have a strong influence on me later in life by teaching me the value of maintaining stability as well as the importance of lasting friendships.

Anyway, when I arrived at Oceanside in the seventh grade I was ready to put my roots down. I made friends with just about everyone in my homeroom. At last I was able to stay in one place, but it didn't happen quite the way I had anticipated. When I was in the eighth grade my father died of a sudden heart attack. He was thirty-nine years old and was a Master Sergeant. He had also been a heavy smoker.

This was in September of 1958 and our lives were to change. Fortunately, because of his pension and Social Security we got by without too many problems. His death actually brought us really closer together as a family and from this experience I have come to realize that when there is love in the family you can survive almost anything. The saying "Love conquers all," in this case speaks to my family and what we went through.

My mother was an incredible woman and she continued to support my sister and me in everyway that she could and, most importantly, even with my father's death we continued to feel her love. We always had a roof over our heads and food. And because of the way mom handled this loss of my dad and because of her ability to survive as a single mom, I realize she set a pattern within me about the value of being a parent. She was the role model I would pattern myself after. Many people sought her advice and she always was a very caring and giving woman. She continued to be this way throughout her entire life.

I remember with fondness and nostalgia the start of each school year. As summer came to what was always a too early and abrupt end, September arrived and it was necessary to buy the year's supply of school clothes. Our ritual, because of the scarcity of large clothing stores in Oceanside, was to drive all the way to Escondido, a distance of twenty miles, to their Sears store. Sears was large enough to have what we needed and it was a store everyone knew you could trust. I can still see myself looking wistfully at the various pants and shirts, trying to figure out which ones would be most appropriate to my tastes. I can even remember the way these new clothes smelled.

There is nothing like the smell of new clothes, especially when you don't get them very often. After my sister and I made our selections, mom gave the final approval. I was very easy and conservative in my selections, but with my sister it was a little more difficult. She had somewhat of a more liberal flare in her desires which mom, of course, had to reconcile. Once the decisions had been made, off we'd go, clothes in hand for another year.

As a pre-teen and teenager, Oceanside was an ideal place to grow up. It was small, much more intimate than it is today. We had complete freedom to go places, day or night, without parents having to worry if someone was going to try to harm us. Oceanside, as everyone was aware, was safe and for a dime you could hop on the bus and go anywhere you wanted. The bus would take you north, south, east and west, and you'd be dropped off within a short five-minute walk of your desired location. We had freedom to roam and be kids, not realizing what a true luxury this was. There was the pier, the longest on the coast, the beach, plenty of natural sand, and a rapidly developing culture of the wave. Surfing was soon to be upon us all.

After junior high school, I entered Oceanside High School with the class of '63. This was in September of 1959. Back then there were no fences, which now encircle the school and provide a dire warning for intruders to keep away. We had an open campus. For lunch, if you so desired, you could leave the campus and eat at the new shopping center that had just opened. This was Oceanside's first real shopping center with three or four different stores. For five cents you could buy a large scoop of ice cream at the Thrifty Drug Store, and for seven cents you could buy a one-quarter pound Baby Ruth candy bar. My favorite!

In high school I was not what you would call a socialite nor was I an introvert. I didn't fit into any one particular group but found myself fitting in with everyone. I remember once going to Gloria Bedwell's house to work on the yearly float and I met her parents, but actually didn't involve myself in many of these extra-curricular types of activities.

I was placed in advanced types of classes, but now realize that I did not extend myself as much as I could have. I remember my freshman class of English where I, and most of the others in the class, disliked the teacher. It was probably one of those mutual things where he felt we weren't responding in a manner fitting to our pre-determined abilities. He gave us an open book final and when he passed back the results everyone flunked. This teacher and his overbearing manner still leave a kind of dour feeling in my stomach. How could that have been that everyone failed an open book test? We were the best of the best! We were the hot shots, but I remember we reciprocated with a kind of student revenge at the end of the year.

The school had a carnival where we could do what was called "purchasing a teacher." In his case, if we purchased him, we could wrap adhesive tape around his leg and slowly yank it off, which of course may have caused him a great deal of pain. The students joined forces and purchased him, and then we took turns yanking the tape off. I'm not sure how much pain this actually caused him, but he feigned a great deal. I became the recipient of this tape, which I held onto for many years, only to discard when it had finally lost its significance.

Mr. Troy was my favorite teacher and he taught my favorite subject, math. In relation to Mr. Troy, I had an experience that still brings out the "hibbi-jibbies" in me and I can't believe what I did. In Oceanside it was common for students to go to Tijuana with their parents and on the return trip they would sneak back with fireworks and firecrackers. And everyone knew that the best ones were the cherry bombs.

Well, I had the good fortune of purchasing a cherry bomb from a friend and pondered what to do with it and how I could best utilize its explosive potential. I brought this cherry bomb to school and kept it in my pocket, wondering if I would have the guts to actually blow it up on campus. I remember taking a furtive look at the cherry bomb as I surveyed the various possible locations, and I could feel my anxiety jump when at last the ideal setting had been found. There was, would you believe, a broken locker close to Mr. Troy's room; his classroom was away from what was considered to be the lunch court. I wandered over to this locker, building up my courage along the way. I checked and double checked to see if anyone was looking, and when all was clear, I lit the cherry bomb, tossed it into the locker, slammed the door and hightailed it out of there.

There was a slight hill, which I charged up. I can still remember my heart pounding and trying to catch my breath. I even momentarily slipped and fell, ripping my Levi's, and as I got to the top of the hill it came: "Ka-Boom!" The cherry bomb blasted the locker and smoke filled Mr. Troy's room. Drops of sweat perched upon my brow as a most interesting thought suddenly occurred to me: *What have I done?* Paroxysms of fear and guilt took hold. Would I get caught? *What would my mother think when the school calls to tell her what I've done? What would Mr. Troy think when he finds out it was me?* With my mind riddled with the awareness of my actions and my body jumping with the electricity and jolts of adrenalin, I joined some friends at the lunch court and casually melted in.

I didn't say anything to anyone about what I had done, and it wasn't long before this incident was forgotten. I got away with it, but I learned I wasn't meant to be a serous prankster. This cherry bomb incident was definitely out of my comfort zone. Now I recognize this as one of the most treacherous things I would ever do in my life. But the result was that I had learned an important lesson about myself and the way I wanted to be.

I attended a few of the most important school activities, football games and basketball games, and there was one football game my senior year that most of us attended. We were to battle the neighboring city of Carlsbad for the CIF championship. We had Terry Scott who we knew was the greatest quarterback Oceanside had ever seen and we were sure he was destined to play in the pros. We had George Mills as the fullback, who many of us considered to be the strongest man alive for his size, and we had an arsenal of fine receivers. How could we lose? Why were we even pitted against this inferior team from Carlsbad?

The game was held on a cold and dreary Friday evening with fog so thick you could cut it with a knife. I, and all of the other spectators, sat there for three hours and didn't actually see one play. But what happened was one for the history books. We lost and our egos had been seriously demoted.

In high school I was considered to be quite a good student, but once I'd graduated I was ready for the real world. College was not something that was considered important by my family. I had already held a part-time job that had ended. Jobs for eighteen year-olds weren't easy to come by and I was doing temporary work through the Oceanside Employment Agency. I got sent out on very difficult jobs, but eventually found full time employment at Marja Acres Eggs in Carlsbad. It was tough, long hours and this was where I learned what work was all about. It was definitely a good experience and after all of these years I still remain friends with those people.

After graduation, I'd decided it was time to change my life style. I'm not going to say that I turned into a total party animal, but there were some dances I attended, and I found I liked to dance, but there was one party that stands out in my mind. Bob Selby, the older brother of Dick Selby who is compiling this book, masterminded this and he and I are friends to this day. The party took place in 1965 out in the hills of what is known as North Carlsbad. Bob sold tickets for two dollars each up and down the coast advertising it as a toga party. "Man," I thought to myself, "this sounds really good. There would be plenty of beer, wine, girls, and several pigs would be roasted." Bob pre-sold several hundred tickets and collected money as people entered. This party was supposed to officially get underway during the late afternoon, but the much awaited enthusiasm and anticipation brought an early start and I was one of the earliest. People were drinking and eating and, as parties frequently seemed to go, two people were already fighting; and by five-thirty in the evening cars could be seen lining up on the highway. This party would be the success everyone had hoped for.

Yes, this was something special and as we talked and drank and partied, a variety of squad cars drove in. Beer, wine, togas, everything was scattered as panic set in and people fled to the hills, only for all of us to be herded back, our names taken and then for us to be released. The following day papers throughout the nation carried this story of Bob's toga party, with girls running around naked when their togas had been ripped off. This party was big news and Bob received clippings from friends back east.

It was quite an experience and for all of us who were there, and though we didn't know it at the time, this party would be one for the books and one to be enjoyed by posterity. Bob has since stated that it was his party that provided the impetus for the toga party in the movie *Animal House*.

From working in Carlsbad, I soon ended up working at Fair View State Hospital in Costa Mesa. It was all because a girl I was dating was working there and I thought: *Hey, I'd kind of like to do this too.* I took the civil service test and got the highest score that anyone had ever received. In my interview for hiring, there was a retired Army nurse named Nurse Bernal and she was hard as nails, kind of like Nurse Krachet in "One Flew Over the Cuckoo's Nest". "Do you know what this job entails?" she queried. "You will have to change diapers on adult males."

Nurse Bernal did her best to grill me and discourage me, but I got the job and found I loved this type of work. I dealt mostly with retarded children and I can still remember many of their names. I worked there for about four years. I was living in Orange County and got married, not with the girl that brought me to Costa Mesa, but with someone else I'd fallen in love with. I was twenty-one years old. This marriage lasted eight years and we had two children. When I think about this marriage now I realize we were too young. We were just kids, and I also believe that men, and I include myself in this, don't really mature until after the age of thirty. But even though the marriage ended, I continued to be a hands-on father always being there as much as possible.

Approximately three years after my divorce I married again. I was thirty-two and this marriage lasted for seventeen years. We had three children and after seventeen years, and when the last child was born, this marriage ended. But I have totally enjoyed being a father and to this day my kids are all most important to me. I just loved being a dad and cherish those experiences we had: camping, sports and just being together

I retired five years ago from sales work where I had been one of the top salespeople in the company for the past twenty-five years. During these years of work, I had become accustomed to fifteen-hour days, working at a fast pace and dealing with a lot of stress. I'm not sure how I handled it as well as I did, but I did and in many ways I liked the action and the responsibilities. Then "boom" I retired and it all ended.

People talk about how great retirement is, but for me it was not as much fun as I had hoped. In fact, I started to find it outright boring. I like to keep myself occupied and have many irons in the fire, and with retirement I was a like a fish out of the water. Then one day a miracle occurred. I was at the ophthalmologist's office getting some new glasses when I read a brochure about an agency in Arizona called "Greater Foothills Helping Hands." Volunteers were needed to help with the elderly. Well, there I was feeling sorry for myself and wondering how I could even make it through the day, and here was a request for volunteers. I thought: *What the heck! I might as well check this out. What do I have to lose?*

I've now been volunteering at Greater Foothills Helping Hands for four years and this is where I find meaning in life. I do a variety of things to help, from taking people to doctors' appointments to minor house repairs. I even helped a lady through chemotherapy. She died, but I was there for her as much as I could be, and as I worked with these people I've come to believe that I get more out of helping them than they get from me. Some have become my good friends and I admire them so much. There's one couple that inspires me about life, about love and about marriage. They have been married for seventy-two years and after all these years he still loves her so much. My eyes water when I see the two of them together and how much they still love one another. I enjoyed my Christmas dinner with them. This was very special.

Helping others is what life is really all about and by doing this we're really helping ourselves. I've been fortunate to assist classmates from our class. In fact, I try to get back to Oceanside whenever I can. We are getting older and some of us are experiencing illnesses from which we might not recover and there are those in the class who have already passed, but we are family. I've learned that it's important to continue being family and to share our lives as we move into our future years.

Yes, I was probably what you would term one of those military brats, changing schools whenever my father got transferred. I didn't start off in Oceanside, but know that when we moved there we were most fortunate. That was approximately fifty-five years ago, but even though I've lived in many other places, Oceanside is now where my roots lie. I find myself returning from my home in Arizona whenever I can.

Yes, it's nostalgia, but for all of us in our class, we grew up in Oceanside when it was really special. Many of those things that we took for granted are no longer there. But high school is a most important time of our lives and we grow up so much.

Over these past fifty years, my classmates and I have seen a lot and done a lot and I know there is much more for us to experience. And even though I'm retired now and my kids are grown, in many ways I don't see myself as slowing down. I'm just doing different things. I'm helping others and being there when I can be of any assistance. This I believe is what we're supposed to be doing. That's the way I am and that's the way I want to continue to be.

CHAPTER 10

Nurse Practitioner of Hope
Judy Stettler Gabler

My father was in the Army and met and married my mother while he was stationed in England. I was born in England on August 25th, 1945. Eight days later the war with Japan ended. My father was among the first to return to the United States and to Oceanside. His return trip was on the Queen Mary, or the Gray Ghost, as it was known during the war. Mom and I followed soon afterwards, also being transported to the United States on the Queen Mary. Mom and I visited the Queen Mary about a year ago and were informed that there are very few of those original passengers alive today.

We lived in South Oceanside and my parents continued living in the same house for the next forty years. My father and uncle had their own plastering business. My cousin Tom, who also has his story included in this book, lived almost directly in back of me for several years.

South Oceanside was an incredible place to grow up. I started my education at South Oceanside Elementary School. Living but two blocks away, I either walked or rode my bicycle to school. The community was safe and parents didn't worry about their children the way they do today. South Oceanside Elementary had a large field and many eucalyptus trees that reached high into the sky, dropping their bark and branches, sometimes in prodigious amounts, to the barren terrain below. Nothing would grow directly underneath the large trees. The play areas were spacious and there were no fences separating the grounds of the school with the surrounding neighborhood. It was easy access from any direction. Now large fences enclose the entire school and most of the eucalyptus trees have long ago been cut down.

In the fifth grade, and this was a remarkable event for the era, I had my first male teacher, Mr. Trainer. Men simply didn't teach elementary school and he was one of the first. The other girls and I thought he was just the handsomest man. Then in the sixth grade, and because of overcrowding, my class was transferred to Laurel Street School. Laurel was in the poorer section of town and it was a big change for everyone. It was comprised mostly of Latinos and African-Americans. It was necessary for the students each morning to meet at the corner of South Oceanside Elementary School and board the bus. The year was 1955 and we represented whites being bused into a minority school, years before the concept of integration had even become a legal consideration. The adjustment was difficult in the beginning, but my father was not overly concerned about this sudden transition. He had worked with many Latinos and had grown to respect them. My mother had similar sentiments and I believe that their attitudes, along with my own personal experiences, influenced me in being both understanding and accepting of all the races.

It took a little time, but the students from South Oceanside Elementary and from Laurel Street became friends. I have the fondest memories of this year, mostly because of my best friend, Linda Austin. She and I formed our own little club, and often would sit on the playground writing stories, drawing, and laughing and laughing. We'd be sitting there, somewhere way out on the furthest section of the playground, and we'd look around...and it would be just the two of us. For some reason, this always came as a surprise. Giggling as we picked up our supplies, we'd rush off, once again to be late. Oh, it was in the sixth grade when we had our first sex education class. Yes, it was now 1956 and we had sex education. This was only for those "mature" sixth grade girls, who of course we all were, and those immature sixth grade boys, who of course they all were, were excluded.

Jefferson Junior High School came next, bringing together the sixth graders from the various elementary schools throughout the city. There was a teacher who left a lasting impression upon me. Her name was Mrs. Freeberg. She was my seventh grade homeroom teacher and to this day she was the best teacher I've ever had. She was truly gifted with what probably would be termed a photographic memory. I remember her reading the *Jungle Book* to us, but actually she didn't read it. She simply looked at the page and was able to repeat it exactly. We couldn't wait for her to sit down and read to us. It was mesmerizing.

Mrs. Freeberg was a large woman and quite fond of wearing tight dresses. One dress was green, and with her red hair cascading over her shoulders, and with her high heels and earrings shinning brightly, she kept us all in a constant state of bewilderment and admiration. There were the times when she'd reach way out and grab and hug you, her large bosoms and shoulders and red hair encasing you, from which there was no escape. I'm still not sure if we were happy when this happened, or terrified? She had a mink stole. I remember her as she walked down the hall, this large bosomed lady with red hair and mink stole, proudly showing the entire world who she was. Everyone loved her, but I was special. I had some artistic skills and did her bulletin boards. I was in seventh grade and in seventh heaven.

The eighth grade was not as special, for who could possibly replace the ineffable Mrs. Freeberg. But there were several important events that happened that year. I remember the day we were on the yard during lunch when this plane buzzed us and then headed off to the nearby canyon; we watched it go into a tailspin and head downwards. We all thought how strange and then a large plume of the darkest black smoke rose from deep within the canyon's interior. Our hearts sank and we stood frozen. Everyone on board was killed. But something of the greatest significance happened while I was in the eighth grade. I started to notice boys. The junior high school ended and I was off to high school and the ninth grade. I had gotten straight "A's" throughout both elementary and junior high school. Life was good.

High school, unfortunately, was to bring a series of emotional challenges and setbacks. From the elation and success of elementary school and Jefferson, I went into a tailspin as I encountered a teacher and a class that was a nightmare. It was my ninth grade English class and the thought of it still brings shivers down my back as well as a slight feeling of nausea. I'd entered high school with enthusiasm and passion. Because of my success I was placed in an honors type of English class where each week we had the most disturbing assignment of giving a three-minute "impromptu" speech. I was terribly shy and stricken with fear because of this one weekly requirement. I could feel my heart pounding and the physical and mental agitation building as my turn in alphabetical order slowly approached, and there was no escape. If

we didn't say anything, we just stood there in silence, suffering in our own personal agony for the full three minutes.

Well it didn't take me long to come up with a solution.
I stood there teary eyed, blushing, and emotionally dev-
astated, counting each second in my mind until the three
minutes were over. Then I would sit down, feeling awful,
but knowing I had survived another week of this teacher's
well-designed torture. And to top it off, he would state
that he was doing this for our benefit. "Speech" he said, "is
a requirement in college." I knew then that if this indeed
were the case, college would not be a part of my future.

Fortunately, that ninth grade came to an end, and
throughout high school there were a few teachers
who were excellent. Mr. Clavier, for tenth grade social
studies, brought the subject alive, and then there was
Mr. Rossbach. Wow! Double wow! He was young,
dynamic, and not too bad to look at. He taught Spanish
and had been true to his discipline. He had even married
a Mexican woman. Mr. Rossbach had graduated from
the University of Mexico and was a body builder, something quite novel at this time, and he'd even garnered the
title of "Mr. Mexico." But this was Oceanside and I was a
teenager coming into my own. I was part and parcel of
the surf, the pier, and the culture of the beach.

The Beach Boys had come on the scene and surf
music was riding a wave of unprecedented success. Dick
Dale and his "Wipe Out" became an instant classic, while
I, in the apogee of my teenage years, frequented various
beaches, especially Oceanside's pier, proudly portrayed
as being the longest pier on the coast. You could buy a
hamburger for thirty-five cents at Mom's Restaurant and
we'd all take bites. We'd share our fries and cokes. The
sixties were upon us and we basked in the sun, hung out,
cruised, and we knew that what we were experiencing

was the way life was meant to be. This really was "Surfing USA." We feasted on our thirty-five cent hamburgers, played hearts and crazy eights, and tanned in the summer sun, not recognizing what this period would represent to future generations. Then along came surf movies.

Bruce Brown was the headliner when he came to Oceanside, filling its community center: "The Endless Summer" and "Surf Crazy," are classics, but there were other movies, narrated live by their producers and I went to them all: "Out of Control," "Going My Wave," "Surfing Wild," and I still have all the posters. In the movie, "The Endless Summer," Bruce Brown showed us the worst wipeout of all time and it was from our very own Danny DeRohan. Danny went to South Oceanside Elementary School and from this movie he instantly became a surfing legend. After the surf movies, there would be the dances and we'd have live bands. These were the best of times and I have come to believe that once the beach and the surf get into your system, you identify with them for the rest of your life: once a surfer girl, always surfer girl, and through it all I was living, loving, and growing up.

I will never forget graduation night. We went to Disneyland and I had a large straw purse. I cut out the bottom and covered it with towels so that I could sneak in several small bottles of booze. These I passed out—no pun intended here, the small bottles of booze to some of my wild and crazy friends, after we'd arrived at Disneyland. We danced, ate, rode some of rides, and in the morning hours, exhausted and drained from the excitement of the previous day, made a weary return. We came back and went out for one last breakfast and that was it. High school was over and those years, the four years that had commandeered my adolescence and innocence, the bravado, the friends, and the tears, had ended. I was about to embark into an entirely new and different world.

I graduated at the age of seventeen, turning eighteen in August of 1963. After graduation, aside from the possibility of marriage, the basic options for girls were quite limited: work for the phone company or go to junior college. Junior college? Well, there wasn't much of a chance of that, not with that speech requirement. And why should I even think about college? No teachers or counselors had ever encouraged me to even consider this as a viable option. High school ended and I, feeling like a duck out of water, waddled along.

A close friend, Margaret Chaney, planned to move to Santa Barbara and I decided to join her. Well, at the last minute she bailed, but my mind was set and I was not to be dissuaded. After all, I was eighteen, fresh out of high school and looking for excitement and everything that my young life had to bring. So, and not to be dissuaded by a few stumbling blocks, I headed off to Santa Barbara. Not long after my arrival, however, I met the man who was to become my husband and we married. Married at eighteen and by nineteen I had a daughter.

Thinking about this now that I'm somewhat older and wiser, I realize how young I was and that I didn't have even the slightest idea about what I was doing. But it was the early sixties and I was simply following the accepted pattern of the day: get married and have a baby. After our daughter was born, money, unfortunately, was in short supply. My husband had his own business and did many things, but his income was hit-and-miss, and frequently it was more miss. It was necessary for me to go to work and help earn money, so I found on the job training as a dental assistance. My sister, who had now joined me in Santa Barbara, went to school to be a licensed vocational nurse.

My son, Glenn, was born three years after my daughter. So there I was, twenty-two years old with two children, and with a husband who wasn't making much money and who wasn't ready for the responsibilities that marriage and children entailed. My life had taken a turn for the worst and was definitely not what I'd planned.

The United States at this time had also become involved in the Vietnam War; student protestors were making headlines. In Isle Vista, where the University of Santa Barbara is located, the students gained national attention when they burned down the Bank of America. Demonstrations and protests were being held throughout the country. While many young men were being injured and dying in Vietnam, with some them from my own high school, I was involved with my own day-to-day living and survival. I was busy being a mother, working one job, trying to make ends meet, and also taking on a few part-time jobs.

My marriage lasted nine years and then came the time to call it quits. In all fairness, we were both too young for the responsibilities that marriage and family responsibilities had brought, and in all fairness we each had much growing up to do.

After the divorce, I was on my own and struggling, and because of my limited finances I qualified for a special program. It was called the "WIN Program" and it was designed to help mothers on welfare with dependent children. The government would pay me to go to school. So at the age of thirty-two I began my training to become a licensed vocational nurse, a career I'd never thought about before, even though my sister was now doing this work. It took eighteen months to complete the course and become licensed, and once I had succeeded I knew I wasn't going to stop. The reality of life and what

I'd experienced had left its mark. I went back to junior college, taking all of the requirements that were necessary to get an AA Degree. I needed this to be eligible to enter the RN program. My biggest concern continued to be that dreaded speech class, but a less stressful class, a conversation type of class served as a substitute, and I was on my way. It took me five years to complete both the AA Degree and the RN program.

I remember coming home in my nursing uniform and doing my best to take care of the family, while simultaneously meeting both the academic requirements and the training. There were nights, after preparing the meals and doing a few other things, I would lie down on the couch and immediately fall asleep. Hours later I would wake up, usually around three in the morning, still wearing my nurse's uniform. It was difficult but I wasn't about to give up. I knew that through these efforts a better life was waiting.

Between the LVN program and the RN program, I met my second husband. We lived together for two years and got married in 1982. I have come to believe that he is my soul mate. Right before we got married he was diagnosed with testicular cancer. I remember when he told me about this cancer and it was shock, but I also knew he was the one for me. My response was: "You're not going to get rid of me that easily. No way." We've now been married almost thirty years.

My daughter, Jennifer, was raised in Carpinteria where we lived for twenty-eight years. She was a bit of tomboy and one day she returned from surfing, telling me that she was the only girl among all of the boys catching the waves. I knew then that she'd become aware of boys and that both her life and ours were about to change, and I was right. She also has what is called A.D.D. (Attention Deficit

Disorder) and back then we didn't know much about it. A year after my second husband and I got married, she married. I became a grandparent at thirty-seven. My son had a few of his own issues, but he has successfully handled them. Sometimes I think that parents learn as much or even more than their own children during this lifetime parenting process. We've now been blessed with eight grandsons and I've recently become a great grandparent. I now have a great grandson.

After working as an RN, I decided to take the next step and become a nurse practitioner. I applied to UC Davis and was accepted into the program for nurse practitioners, which I started at the age of forty-five. I completed the program when I was forty-seven and have been working as a nurse practitioner for twenty years.

My husband had worked in recreation, but went back to school and became an elementary school teacher. With these two incomes, we were then in a position to buy a house, but not in Santa Barbara. They're just too expensive there. I had a brother who was living in northern California and we decided to move to the city of Willits. There we were able to purchase a beautiful home on twenty acres for $167,000.

We've made one more change and that was to Nevada City, which we did about six or seven years ago. My daughter lived there and I felt it was important to be close to her. Her second son had died around this time; he'd had a heart condition that went uncorrected. I was very close to this grandson and with his passing I wanted us to be together as family. There are many places to camp and hike in the area, which we enjoy, and we know that being with family is most important to us.

I currently work as a nurse practitioner three days a week and I see many people who have no medical insurance. I work at the "Chapa-de Indian Health Clinic" in family practice. I work with Native-Americans and I believe this is my calling. I also believe my experiences in Oceanside and at Laurel Street School helped me to feel comfortable with people of all races. In this clinic we don't deny services to anyone and the Native-Americans we serve are mostly from the Maidu Tribe. Many are poor and depressed and feel there is little hope. I know that because of things I've experienced I can give them that hope. With what I've gone through, in many ways I've been in the same position in which they find themselves. I was a single mother on welfare and food stamps and went back to school. I can relate to these people because of their circumstances and I feel a great sense of satisfaction from working there.

But being a nurse practitioner is demanding and the most difficult aspect is the search for medical care for people who don't have sufficient medical insurance. I've come to believe that our health care system as it functions right now is great if you have good coverage, a Cadillac comprehensive kind of coverage, but it's pathetic if you do not. I know there are many countries in the world that offer excellent health care to all their citizens and this is what we need to do. Health care is a human right and it is not something that should be subjective and denied because of a lack of adequate insurance. Our health care is based on profit and that is wrong. Everyone deserves good health care.

Currently I'm looking forward to retirement. It's time to be a wife and a grandmother, and I want to do things that I haven't had time to do, like art and gardening. I know this will happen, but with the economics of today it may take a little longer than I had thought; we are experiencing our own unexpected economic difficulties.

But through it all, my husband and I have worked at our marriage and we have fun, laugh, and can tell each other anything without the threat of anger or retaliation. We are able to focus on the present and the pertinent issues. We also have a deep respect for each other and have used our relationship as a way to reach out and help others. We've trained in seminars, and for someone such as myself who previously experienced tremendous fear about speaking in front of groups this has come as a welcomed change.

My husband and I believe that we have been able to achieve this level of satisfaction because of an important experience going back to the seventies. There was a well-known, but quite controversial series of seminars known as EST (Erhard Seminar Training). Some people thought of it as brain washing, but basically it taught a way to look at life and our experiences. It is now known as the Landmark Forum. I remember several hundred people gathering in a large auditorium and for sixteen hours we were together and during this time we weren't permitted to go to the bathroom. EST became famous because of this requirement. But this program taught people to take responsibility for their own actions and not to blame others. It taught people to focus on the present and to not get sidetracked by the kinds of mental stories that we create. And perhaps most importantly, it taught the philosophy that we are in charge of our lives and that we have the power within ourselves to be happy. Happiness is our right! Yes, EST was controversial, but it provided my husband and I with a framework for looking at the world. It taught us to avoid the emotional traps that prevent so many people from realizing their own potential and of finding happiness. It was this training that helped gave me the confidence to push myself beyond my own self-imposed limits.

It's now been almost fifty years since high school and when I look back on my life I remember my adolescence and Oceanside with a special kind of fondness. There was the beach, friends, and an innocence and enchantment that pervaded the beach, the sixties, and those most important teenage years.

Yes, I consider myself fortunate to have grown up in Oceanside and to have these many wonderful, difficult, and challenging experiences. And I know the time is coming when I'll have to say goodbye to my nursing career, which I love so much, and move into a different setting. But Judy Stettler Gabler, the surfer girl with all of the original movie posters, can look back to her life and family with pride. This has been a fantastic life and one worth living. And when I think about it, I wouldn't want it any other way.

CHAPTER 11

The Right Mental Framework
Tomas Romero, RCE

The opportunity to talk about my life and give my story has reminded me of how fortunate I have been. My childhood and my earliest living situation was a little different than most of my classmates, but I think the differences have helped me to have a clearer understanding of some of the important issues society is dealing with today. I moved to Oceanside from Nicaragua during the sixth grade and when I arrived I didn't speak any English. I was a total non-English speaker.

Before going into my experiences here in the United States, I want to give you some history on Nicaragua. I believe that this history will give you an understanding of the living conditions that we were faced with while we were in Nicaragua and, hopefully, you will understand why it was so important for us to come here.

When we emigrated from Nicaragua it was the typical "banana" republic that you found in Central and South America. It was a politically unstable country ruled by a small, self-elected, but wealthy group of individuals with its primary economic reliance on a few agricultural products. Chiquita Banana, United Fruit Company and others thrived on the cheap labor and the multiple crops that were available. Nicaragua, however, is also blessed with a variety of other natural resources. Gold and silver as well as lumber are important natural resources and these were exported in large quantities to the Allies during World War II. Most of the profits from these resources, unfortunately, were funneled to a few select individuals in power who controlled everything.

Nicaragua's political instability began in 1909 when American troops invaded and set up a puppet government to maintain control of that region. There was a constant fluctuation of control and political leaders until Somoza Garcia came to power in 1936. He was a despot out for his own best interests, but was able to maintain his control because of the direct support from the United States. In 1956, twenty years after he came to power, he was assassinated. As the saying goes, "The king is dead, long live the king," and his two sons took over. Nothing in the country changed. The eldest son, a US trained engineer became president while the other, a West Point Graduate took charge of National Guard. Political instability, poverty, high unemployment, and a general state of discontent continued to exist throughout the country.

Because of the economic and political environment that existed, my parents realized that if they could move to the United States it would be best for all of us. (My father, who was trained as both a barber and a tailor, had temporarily moved to Panama where he could find work. He was unable to find work in Nicaragua because of the political environment.) The United States held promise for a newer and better life, and the immigration policy in those days was quite different than it is today. According to the immigration policy of the time, if an immigrant was able to show that he could successfully live here without relying on the state, he could legally immigrate and then he could bring over his family.

My father came to the United States in 1955, a year before the rest of us. He was originally to have a job in New York, but when that didn't materialize his second choice, which he termed plan "B," was set into motion. He came to Oceanside and was able to obtain employment in Camp Pendleton as a barber. My mother, sister and I moved here in 1956.

In the beginning it was very difficult for us. Major changes are always going to be somewhat traumatic and that was certainly the case with us. Our first apartment was completely inadequate with all of us being crammed into a one-bedroom apartment. And then, unfortunately, there was this thing called the English language, which none of us spoke.

My parents encouraged my younger sister and I to learn English as quickly as possible and the process they devised was quite simple. My father had purchased several Berlitz records and he insisted that we listen to these records for a couple of hours each day. I hated doing this and I'm not sure that it made any difference in my actual acquisition of the language, but both my sister and I did listen and repeat as instructed. I realize now through my own experiences that to become totally fluent in a language takes a long, long time and listening to these records was simply a beginning. In retrospect, both of my parents understood how important it was for my sister and I to become fluent English speakers and we, too, soon realized its importance.

I entered school at Ditmar Avenue Elementary School and was immediately assigned a student from the class to help with my initial adjustment. His name was Jim Miller and it was his task to show me around and give me the basics, and I know this: Not knowing the language, coming into a new culture, and not having friends is one of the most difficult and emotionally stressful situations that a person can experience. Jim "showed me the ropes" and though we certainly didn't know it at the time, we were destined to become friends and we've remained so to this day. In fact, he was my best man at my wedding 30 years ago. (Other friends I'd made in Oceanside, Bruce McDonald and George Mills, both from the class of 1963, have kept in touch and we've even participated in each others wedding.)

In this process of learning a new language, making friends and adjusting to the American culture, my math background proved to be beneficial. In Nicaragua there was an early emphasis on math. I'd actually had some Algebra and even some basic Trigonometry in the fourth and fifth grades before coming here. This advanced early preparation helped me to feel, even though I was struggling with the language, that I could be successful. In junior high, and I believe this was quite significant for me at the time, my math teacher, Mr. Yossa, singled me out and had me helping him grade papers. Here I was fairly new to the country and what would be classified today as limited English proficient, but grading these papers helped me believe that eventually I could compete with others. I know that this somewhat insignificant act of having me help grade his math papers is something that I feel good about to this very day. It had a direct and positive effect upon my self-confidence.

In high school my language skills continued to improve and I was successful in most areas, but in English class I still felt that I was at somewhat of a disadvantage. I would just sit quietly in class and not say a word. I felt intimidated, but in the other classes I didn't feel this same type of intimidation and self-imposed restraint. In tenth grade history, for example, with Mr. Clavier, and in the math classes with Mr. Troy, my reactions were entirely different, and in both of these classes I did really well. In fact, Mr. Troy was a teacher that set the standard on how math should be taught. He was fantastic and it's amazing how to this day I am impressed with how he presented the material. He made it clear, concise, and understandable, and I believe that it was because of his influence that I eventually went into engineering. I've now had many teachers in math, but he was the best.

Looking back to my adjustment to Oceanside and to my classes, one issue that I dealt with, and this is strictly in today's way of thinking, was that I came into Oceanside as a minority. But Oceanside High School because of Camp Pendleton and also because of its proximity to the border was its own kind of natural melting pot. We had a mixture of all the different races and cultures (white, African-American, Latino, Asian, Samoan) and within this mixture I made friends with everyone.

I also know that I never thought of myself as being a minority or of being different. I didn't see myself this way and because I didn't internalize these feelings, I don't think others saw me any differently either. I've also come to believe, based on my own personal experiences, that it is counter productive when someone views themselves as different or inferior because they are or a different race. I don't think it helps in the long run and it can affect how an individual feels about himself.

I am stating these things because I know what I went through as I went from a non-English speaker to a fluent English speaker, and as I progressed through the different levels of education. I think it begins with self-honesty. We need to be clear about what our abilities are, and then we need to be clear about our goals. Are these two in line with each other and compatible? And if this is the

case, as we proceed we're all going to experience difficulties, but we shouldn't let them stop us. We need to
keep going. Fortunately, I was able to develop some of
these philosophical ideas about life and what it takes to
be successful when I was in high school. I was fortunate to
have a mentor, someone to guide me in my thinking, and
it was Pat Downey, the assistant director of the Oceanside
Boys Club.

It was in the early sixties, in my junior year when I got
a job working at the Oceanside Boys Club. Pat Downey
was the assistant director and coach, and he encouraged several of us to become involved in weightlifting.
Pat was one of those early enthusiasts about the benefits
of lifting weights, not just for us but for himself too, and we
could see how strong he had gotten. Weightlifting at this
time was just beginning to become popular and some
friends from the class of '63, including Masa Mayeda,
Bruce McDonald, George Mills and myself, led the way.
We were young and energetic, and as we lifted weights
each week we could see ourselves improve. Eventually we
formed a team and off we would go to competitions. We
got quite good my senior year and early college years.
George actually won first place in a power lifting competition for his weight category for all of California. And
I set a state record in the bench press for my weight division... that lasted for all of five minutes. But I'm proud of
that accomplishment. And then there was Tommy Badillo,
who was a couple of years younger than us. He weighed
123 pounds and bench-pressed 315 pounds. When I think
back on this we were quite an amazing group of young
power lifters.

Pat was the organizer, the one who had gotten us
started. But for him it was more than lifting weight and
going to competitions. He was concerned about teaching

us the right mental approach not only to competition, but also to life. He taught us to keep going and to reach our potential. He guided us not only in how to deal with competition, but with frustration and to work through failure and difficulties. "Life has its ups and downs," he would say, "but don't get overly upset by this. Keep going." Eventually Pat left Oceanside and went to Huntington Beach where he was in charge of two Boys' Clubs.

The weight training taught me self-discipline and the mental approach helped me to deal with any obstacle that might come my way. I can definitely say that as we go through life we are sure to meet a few obstacles on the path.

After high school, I went to Mira Costa College in Oceanside and then transferred to San Diego State where I majored in engineering. I know that Mira Costa College provided me with an excellent education and when I left there I felt totally prepared to attend San Diego State. I'm saying this because I know for my friends and I, as we took our classes there, the education was excellent. Most of the teachers were good and they cared about what they were doing, but I was fortunate to have one of the finest teachers of my life at Mira Costa and it was Dr. Bockian. He taught chemistry. He had written his own book and made chemistry easy for me to understand. But I also was able to go to him for help in calculus and he had this same ability in calculus, just as he did in chemistry, to make it easy and understandable. Yes, when I left Mira Costa College I felt completely prepared for the academics that lay ahead of me at San Diego State. Unfortunately, there were other issues with which we were dealing at this time.

The country was involved with the Vietnam War and it had demanded the attention and the resources of the entire nation. I had registered for the draft, even though

I wasn't a citizen at this time but was a legal resident. Anyway, it was the mid to the late sixties and college students, such as I, were given a temporary student deferment. Several friends and my brother-in-law were already in ROTC, and immediately after college they went into the service, mostly the Marines, and later they went to Vietnam.

Well, in 1968 my student deferment expired and I was drafted. This was at a time when hundreds of thousands of Americans were already serving in Vietnam. I did my basic training and remember that there were several others from the north San Diego County area going through the training with me. Basic training, for anyone who hasn't experienced it, is quite stressful, both emotionally and physically. Physically, there was a constant emphasis on endurance types of running, physical training, and physical agility types of movements, but I had been a serious power lifter. The kind of weight training that I had done was counterproductive to what was required in the military and my body reacted negatively. I ended up losing about twenty pounds in just a couple of weeks. When I lost all of this weight my back, which had been somewhat of a problem previously, became much more problematical. I couldn't do the physical training that was required. I couldn't run and I even had trouble walking. I was in constant pain. Well, as it turned out the Army didn't want me with these kinds of physical limitations and I ended up going out on a medical discharge; and maybe I was lucky? Others from north San Diego County and from throughout the United States were going to Vietnam, some to be injured or even killed. I was released back to civilian life.

After I was given my medical discharge, rather than go directly back to school, I decided to test the waters and see if I could find work at the entry level utilizing the skills and knowledge that I'd already acquired. I looked around and was hired by the Rick Engineering Company. I knew that I hadn't completed my engineering degree but I was able to get a job that I liked, and on top of that I was making pretty good money. I was happy, financially sound, and things were definitely going my way.

Unfortunately, life frequently has surprises and I was about to get one. In 1975 the nation was going through a slow period economically and I was released from the company. Though losing my job was emotionally very stressful for me, in retrospect it was probably the best thing that could have happened. I went back to school and finished my engineering degree at San Diego State in 1977. Then I went on to pass the state exams to become a Professional Engineer in Civil Engineering. Life brings us surprises, but frequently things that we think are bad for us actually turn out for the best.

I've now worked as a Registered Civil Engineer for over thirty years, working for private companies. Usually this has been in some type of consulting position where my expertise is utilized throughout the entire process. Some of the projects I've worked on have been worth many millions of dollars.

It's been really amazing how the whole thing functions. The process begins when the client/land owner hires a team, which he is required to do. The team is all part of the private engineering company where I work and we've worked together on many different projects. A civil engineer, like myself, prepares a tentative map that shows how this property is to be subdivided, in accordance with how the client wants to use the land... into single-family lots, multi family, commercial and/or industrial. The team is comprised of the following: Soils Engineer, Traffic Engineer, Architect, Planner, Land Use Attorney, EIR consultant (Environmental Impact Report), Landscape

Architect and others. You can see that it is quite complex and that there is much that goes into the project way before any development begins.

As a team we then go before the planning department of the specific city/county where the development is to occur to answer any questions that they may have. Concerns can range from environmental implications, traffic issues, what kind of businesses are going to be opening up, and so on. There can be almost an endless array of questions, but in regard to this I feel I've been most fortunate. The people I've worked with all have good attitudes, excellent problem-solving skills, and we've been able to work together as a cooperative and goal-focused unit.

The initial plan is approved, and this can be a painstakingly slow process, and then we draw up the final plans, incorporating the necessary changes. But after doing this we're not done yet. We then must obtain the final approval from the City/County Engineer, and when we have that we can begin construction on the project. We take our plans and go from what is raw land to a finished product for public use. It is a long, drawn out process with every step being necessary and time consuming, but to see that end result, to see what finally has transpired, is truly rewarding. I'm just one piece of the final puzzle, but I consider myself most fortunate to be that piece.

I've continued to work on a part-time basis, but will be returning to a full time position. I consider myself most fortunate to have been able to involve myself in this type of work because it is something that I love. I'm also at a time in my life where my education and work experiences are beneficial and I can continue to work in a manner that is comfortable for me.

It is because of this rather unique position that I find myself in, and because I am an immigrant to the United

States, I have some thoughts about what it takes to be successful. First, in the United States you can do whatever you want but education is important. The more education you can get, the better. Keep going! Don't give up! Everyone has to deal with classes in school where they have difficulties. I did. I was not one of those straight "A" students, but I worked hard. I don't believe there is such a thing as failure. We need to learn from our difficulties, make the necessary adjustments, and keep going.

I've also come to believe even more strongly in my later years that there are people who have had an important influence and who have helped guide and mentor us. Pat Downey of the Boys' Club was one of these for me. He encouraged me and got me into weightlifting and that helped build my self-esteem. But it was his mental coaching that was most enduring. He was convinced, and he convinced me, that you could do and accomplish just about anything you wanted. It's important to be focused on your goal and to even see yourself as achieving that goal. If we can do this, if we are able to see ourselves accomplishing this goal, the mind and body have a way of guiding us to it. His mental approach has helped me when I've faced those areas of difficulty and to keep going.

Looking back on my life and all of my experiences, I am grateful for Pat Downey and the Boys Club. For the last thirty years, I've been helping out with Boys and Girls Clubs. I volunteer as a director. I'm not in charge of the clubs, but help raise money so that they can operate. Each year we have a dinner to celebrate the "Man of the Year," someone who has dedicated himself to helping others and serving in the community. This is an important event and we've been able to raise thousands of dollars to help support Boys and Girls Clubs in San Diego. I am also involved in interviewing graduating high school seniors who apply for the Spence Reese Scholarship. This scholarship is over-seen by the San Diego Boys and Girls Club office.

And last, but not least, over the years I've learned to appreciate my bilingualism. Being bilingual helps you to function in situations and to relate to people when others are unable to do so. This has been especially important my last seven years of work, which have been in the County of Imperial where eighty percent of the people are bilingual. Many of the meetings, conferences, and even presentations are held in English, Spanish, or both. Each language is beautiful, but each language also expresses a certain cultural aspect. It is because of this cultural aspect that bilingualism gives you a different and I believe more complete perspective on life. You are better able to see and understand the thinking process of people, why they react as they do, and it helps you to understand some of the underlying emotional issues.

When I arrived here in 1956 there was just one method of language acquisition, the "sink or swim" method. Everything was taught in English and it was difficult and challenging, but for me it worked. Because I was success-ful, however, doesn't mean it will work the same for oth-ers. We're all different and schools now have a variety of methods to teach non-English speaking students. As to what method works best, I will let my wife and sister answer that one. They are both bilingual educators in San Diego.

Yes, schools have made many improvements over these past fifty years, but one thing that can't be improved upon was my experience at Oceanside High School. It was a wonderful time for me. When I look back on my life, as I've told my two boys now that they have both finished college, these four years that I had at Oceanside High School were some of the best years of my life.

My wife, sons and I returned to Nicaragua in 1993. After the earthquake that they had on September 1972, and the "Contra" war that lasted 10 years, the country was in desperate shape. Not many of the buildings had been rebuilt and there was very high unemployment because the foreign help after the earthquake had gone into the pockets of the people in power. For me, it was very depressing to be there.

Masa Mayeda, George Mills, Bruce McDonald and I were all members of the class of '63 and we all became involved in weightlifting. George was a naturally strong guy who wrestled and was a star on the football team. He went on to play on the Mira Costa College championship team of 1963 as well as at Pomona College. Bruce McDonald used weightlifting to augment football and track where he threw the shot. Bruce continues to compete in master's track and field meets to this day. Masa passed in 1975.

My wife and I attended Pat Downey's funeral about five years ago. Diabetes had gotten the best of him. At the memorial service we listened to many young men and women share what a wonderful influence Pat had been on them. It was especially touching when several eight and nine year-olds got in front of this audience. They shared what a caring, compassionate, and understanding man Pat had been to them and how he had influenced their lives. I was very proud to find out we were able to share Pat with these kids.

CHAPTER 12

Sunbeam and the History House
Nancy Boyer

Every morning when I get up, I open the windows and look out to the Pacific Ocean stretching before me. I see the coastline and its waves and surfers anxiously awaiting their next ride. There's the pier, people strolling casually along the sand, and sunbeams as they glisten across the horizon. A smile crosses my face as I recall my college days and the name my friends had once declared was mine, "Sunbeam." I stand in silent awe to all of this. What will happen on this day? Who will I see and what sort of an impact will I have?

Then as I breath in, I say to myself, "Good morning, God. Do you need any help today?" The fresh ocean air feels good and I can now proceed. This is my daily pattern and I think it has its roots in how I was raised, specifically relating to my mother. Her approach to life was one of kindness and compassion for all. "Each of us is a child of God," she said. "We're all part of His creation."

Mom was an elementary school teacher in both Oceanside and Carlsbad. I remember how committed she was to teaching and how she did whatever she could to provide for each student's individual needs. She loved her students, and the students, well they loved her, too. There are still times, though they are not as frequent nowadays, when her students, adults all of them, talk with me about what a fine teacher she was and how she helped and guided them.

I have a cousin, Harry Zimmerman, who has also had a positive influence throughout my life. Harry was one of the original surfers in Southern California, surfing during the 1940's and 50's when the boards weighed some seventy pounds. There's a picture of Harry in Oceanside's surfer museum, but even though he's older now, he continues to serve as my role model. His philosophy that I, too, have adopted is this: "Make us mindful of the needs of others."

I mentioned my mother, but actually both parents guided me along the right path, and I know I was most lucky to have them. I'm saying this not just because they provided me with the constant awareness that I was wanted and loved, but also because they were comfortable in the fact that I was not their own birth child. I am adopted and I learned of this at an early age. Many adoptive parents are hesitant or even fearful about telling their adopted child that they are not the natural parents, but honesty is important, along with love. My parents were happy to have me and this was something that I always knew.

I was born in 1945, a time when the nation was still involved with World War II. These were hard times and many infants, and this happened for a variety of reasons, were put up for adoption. I was adopted through Dr. Hoskins, who ran a medical practice here in Oceanside. I have a friend in the class on 1963 who was also adopted through Dr. Hoskins. We've shared our opinions and good fortune on how this turned out for each of us. He, too, was raised in a loving family and has done quite well for himself.

When I was growing up I had an adopted brother who was eight years my senior. Eight years is a significant difference and I remember back to the various times when I was fearful of him. It was very difficult having him as a brother, and even though we were raised in the same family, our lives and the kinds of things we did and accomplished were quite dissimilar. He consistently struggled in school and was what I believe could be termed as a sociopath. He was self-centered, had shallow feelings for others, and seemed not to have the normal conscience development in regard to his actions. I also remember that he took very little responsibility for his behavior. He got married and ran off to Florida. His sudden exodus was an immediate relief for me, but it was also one that turned into tragedy. The marriage didn't work out and his wife left him. My brother returned to where she was living and killed both her and one of her girlfriends. Then he put the shotgun to his own head. This was the kind of thing that you never forget.

My personal philosophy on life, and it is a reflection not just because of this, but in the many types of things that I've experienced, is that we need to learn from what happens to us, both the good and the bad. I believe that it is important for each of us to take responsibility for our actions and our lives, and it is only by doing this that we can successfully meet the challenges that we will face along life's path.

I have done my best to take this self-responsibility and to look at the positives of whatever happens to me, but I also recognize that throughout my life I've been very blessed. One of these blessings, and it has been a mainstay for me, has been my natural love of sports. I have just always been physically active. I can remember back to when I was four, and even then I seemed to have a fondness for those things that required physical exertion. And by my sixth birthday this fascination/interest/love of mine had clearly taken root into what would be a lifetime pattern, which to this day I follow. My dad asked me what I wanted for this sixth birthday. I could have the highly sought after "Betsy-Wetsy Doll" that all the girls my age soulfully desired, or a baseball glove. I, rather surprisingly, chose the baseball glove and life has never been the same. And in regard to that baseball glove, some of my most cherished memories are when my father and I went out to the front yard and played catch. This love of sports was unconsciously reinforced by dad's own love of sports. An example of this was when he took me to football games at the high school where we watched, along with many thousands of others, C.R. Roberts score touchdown after touchdown. C.R. lived nearby and had a nephew, Johnny Roberts, who was in elementary school with me. C.R. Roberts was one of the greatest athletes to attend Oceanside High School and was destined for USC. He later played for the San Francisco 49ers and I had the good fortune of again meeting him at the all-city class reunion. He's a really wonderful man.

Elementary school proved to be an enjoyable experience, both in and out of the classroom. Academics, fortunately, were relatively easy for me. And when I wasn't in the classroom I could frequently be found playing sports along with the boys. I think it could safely be said that I quite comfortably filled the role of being a tomboy.

Jefferson Junior High School came next. One important memory was the lunchtime dances. As an emerging adolescent/pubescent girl who was beginning to burst at the seams, I was more than ready for the music to begin. Who would be the first to the dance floor? Who would have the courage to dance the slow ones? Who would dance the fast ones? Which boy would ask me to dance? There were always so many unanswered questions, but as I stood waiting I knew that I was ready. After all, I'd gone through Oceanside's junior high school initiation rite of cotillion. With girls wearing their Sunday best, and boys decked out in white shirts and tie, we'd nervously await instruction in dance and the social graces. For boys, proper etiquette was, "May I have this dance?" And the girls were expected to oblige, and then the boys would bow and the girls would curtsy. This was the way it was to be done. As I stood there on the junior high school dance floor, I knew that I was well prepared for whatever the music and the day's offering would bring. This was excitement at its best.

Unfortunately, junior high is a kind of topsy-turvy experience and for me, too, all was not peaches and cream. Jefferson did bring forth its "ups and its downs." There was the time that another girl and I got beaten up. It started in the bathroom of the girls' gym when we were in P.E., and I'm not sure what was the cause, but whatever it was, it was one of those experiences you would never forget. This very large and much stronger girl, whose name was Sharon, got mad and came after the two of us. To this day, I know that she was the toughest girl on the Jefferson campus. Sharon stuffed each of us behind a toilet, my friend behind one and me behind the other. Somehow we extricated ourselves, tears and all, only to find ourselves sitting in the vice principal's office where we cried hysterically. The vice principal wanted to know why my friend and I were so upset and we tried our best to explain. We were then released back to our classes and that was the end of it. And the other girl, well, there's more to come.

The three of us were still together in physical education and later that year Sharon and I were placed on the same softball team. Sharon played first base and I played third. Sharon was not only big and strong, but she was quite a good athlete. I picked up the hits and threw them to first, where Sharon caught the hardest thrown balls and held her ground. Victory after victory was ours. Junior high ended on a happy note and it was off to the big leagues, high school.

It was early September 1959 as I walked to school with my good friend, Sande Vitkovic, who was a year ahead of me. In fact, we are still best friends. We made our way to our first day of class and I was ready for everything that Oceanside had to offer: dances, football, basketball, and, yes, even the classes. Juniors and seniors roamed proudly and confidently throughout the campus, while most of the ninth graders, including me, looked and acted some-what bewildered as we searched for our classes

I choose sixth period P.E. The Girls' Athletic Association, known simply as "GAA," was during sixth period and this was what most of the better athletics selected. For us girls, there would be no organized interscholastic activities. Girls were considered to be the weaker sex, needing to be protected from the rigors of hard athletics and unhealthy exhaustion. Doctors, mostly men, were truly concerned about the ill effects that could be caused by such manly and physically exhausting activities.

Anyway "GAA" was designed to fill in the void and most of us had been together since junior high school. We formed our own team and Sharon, now one of my best friends, played a prominent role. During my sophomore year, Sharon moved and when she left I cried. I felt as though I'd lost one of my best friends.

High school, however, was not all fun and games and sixth period P.E. We had to study and there were a variety of majors from which to choose. I was a college prep major. I took all of those required classes for college (math, language, science and so on) but Mr. Troy for

Trigonometry and Algebra Two was the best. French class, however, with Mrs. Turnbull proved to be the most significant. I ended up taking four years of French, and now, through the marriage of a cousin, I have French relatives. *Parlez-vous francais? Oui, je parle francais.*

For the most part, high school was smooth sailing, but life, along with time and circumstances have a way of challenging us and causing change. It was October 1962, the beginning of my senior year and we experienced the Cuban Missile Crisis. In the United States we had lived with tension between the world's two super powers, known as the Cold War. But in Oceanside we were to witness first hand Camp Pendleton as it mobilized for a national emergency. The Marines disappeared from the downtown streets. They were gone and Oceanside took on the appearance of a ghost town. War, a nuclear holocaust between the United States and Russia, was a possibility

The extent of the mobilization that we in Oceanside witnessed was the surest and most immediate sign of our danger. Masses of heavy-duty equipment were transported via the freeways and by rail. Camp Pendleton's Del Mar Boat Basin was the destination as this equipment and these young men were deployed for duty. My respect for these Marines went through a complete metamorphosis as I realized the role they played and this threat we were facing. These young Marines were putting their lives on the line for all of us. They were headed into a battle where they might not return. Never again would I take them lightly. The Cuban Missile Crisis ended after eight days but my respect for them would remain. Vietnam was just around the corner.

After high school, I matriculated to the University of Redlands. It is a small, private Baptist university and academically it is rated quite well. I believe that in it academic standing it rates somewhere along with Stanford. We had approximately fourteen hundred students and I ended up with both German and History as my majors.

During my sophomore year, and just as I turned twenty, I spent a semester studying abroad in Salzburg, Austria. After the semester ended, five of us worked during the summer in a factory in Munich. One Sunday, we decided to take the train to Dachau and visit one of the Nazi concentration camps. We wanted to see for ourselves what the Nazis had done. This experience gave me a better understanding of World War II and why it was so important for us to be involved.

When we disembarked in Dachau, there were no signs that would guide us to the concentration camp, so we began our search and just started walking. We wondered if we were even headed in the right direction, when along came this big, red Pontiac convertible, loaded with American servicemen. It stopped and the servicemen asked us what we were doing. "We're looking for Dachau," we told them and they volunteered to take us. We all crowded in. (One of these girls ended up marrying one of these servicemen.)

We arrived at Dachau and got out of the car. Even from the outside it was eerie to look at, but it turned out to be worse that anything I could have imagined. I went through the room that had gas fixtures in the ceiling and could no longer contain myself. I went out and threw-up. These gas fixtures were shaped like sprinklers and every time I see any type of ceiling sprinkler I flash back to Dachau. Dachau. After more than twenty years since its liberation, the smell of burning human flesh from the large ovens still remained. The horror that I witnessed, as well as the inhumanity that the Nazi's had done, affected me to my core and to my soul.

Dachau brought me face to face with the Holocaust, the persecution and the mass murders/genocide of the Jews by the Nazis. And as a result of what I'd witnessed, it was incomprehensible for me to understand the German people, all of them, during these years when this genocide was being carried out. I heard various people claim innocence... that they didn't know what was happening. How could these people not know? There were the trains that carried Jews in cattle cars to the more than ten thousand concentration camps within Germany and to their deaths. I saw Dachau. I saw the ovens and the room where the gassing occurred. I know and I will not forget.

When I returned to Redlands, the Vietnam War was escalating. The draft was closely tracking every eligible male with hundreds of thousands finding themselves in Southeast Asia. I even had a female friend named Gerry who received an induction notice.

The political unrest was tearing the nation apart, but Redlands, and I was glad it was this way, was not a participant in this discord. Fellow students and friends from Oceanside had already been deployed to Vietnam and some did not return. Two friends, Chris Garcia and Daryl Crum, were both killed in Vietnam. Other classmates and young men from throughout the nation were being killed or wounded, while the Marines from Camp Pendleton were occupying the front lines. I supported our young men and our country, but I was soon to come face to face with those who did not share my beliefs and my values.

After Redlands, I went to University of California at Riverside. I had hopes of continuing my graduate studies in history and even obtaining my Ph.D., but almost immediately I knew I was at the wrong place at the wrong time. Riverside's emphasis was not on learning and creating a quality Ph.D. program, but was concerned primarily on organizing and protesting the Vietnam War. What was I doing there? I supported our troops and our nation. Reluctantly, but also knowing it was the right thing for me to do, I dropped out. This has been a decision that I have never regretted.

With graduate studies and the prospects of a Ph.D. no longer my consideration, I needed to start a new and different life. I needed to make some money, but how? But where? A nearby shopping center seemed like a good place to start and BINGO! I was interviewed by the Broadway Department Stores and was accepted into their training program. I remember, prior to actually start-ing work, driving in my VW bug to the important interview and only having thirty cents for gas. I filled the car up and made it there with gas to spare.

I eventually became a buyer of children's clothing. The Broadway provided me with the opportunity to develop and succeed outside of the secluded and protected environment of the educational system, and it was a wel-comed respite. I was tired of going to school, burned out, and needed to involve myself in the real world. I worked at the Broadway for eight years, enjoying my work and gaining expertise in what I was doing. However, in 1976, my father had been diagnosed with both diabetes and cancer, so on a temporary basis I left my job and returned to Oceanside. Oceanside, however, was where I would remain. There would be no more major moves and with Oceanside now as my permanent home, I decided that it was time for me to get involved directly in city govern-ment. From the 70's until the early 90's, I took an active role in Oceanside politics and government, serving on several committees, including the Oceanside Planning Commission. Then the time came when it was time to let others take over this role of politics and city government and I returned to a less involved political life. It was a wel-comed change, but I also left feeling satisfied about the role that I had played.

My father lived for many more years, but mom sud-denly passed in the fall of 1980. Dad was heartbroken and frail, but did his best to meet the many challenges. I believe he was the most courageous man I'd ever met. Then there came a time when even his courage began to fail: "Dad," I told him, "you took care of me when I wasn't able to care for myself, after I came out of the incubator. So now it's my turn to care for you." In 1991 he died. After his death, I maintained the family business, but it had out-lived its profitability. In 1997, I closed it.

Our laundry business (Personal Service Laundry) had been in operation for sixty-seven years and was built in what now constituted the core area of downtown Carlsbad. Up until the City of Carlsbad incorporated in 1952, Personal Service Laundry had been a full laundry plant. It had a boiler, washers and extractors and was designed to handle large amounts of laundry, but the needs of society had changed.

It was time to sell. In 2005, before the recession was to take its toll and deplete the values of much of the real estate, I sold it. It was then demolished to the bare ground and even underneath the ground. Bulldozers knocked down the walls and large dump trucks carried away the remnants. In its place has been built a multi-use devel-opment with an upscale French style restaurant called "Paon," along with offices, residential condominiums, and retail shops. Personal Service Laundry is all gone, but my memory and a few pictures of the way it used to be live on. In fact, Carlsbad's local television just showed a pic-ture of our family business, and there proudly stood my parents.

Today I live in exactly the same house where I grew up. It was built in 1895 and has been in the family since 1918 when my grandparents purchased it. As I walk through the house I imagine the many changes that it has seen: the motorcar, airplanes, two world wars, television, and recently cell phones, HDTV, and the wonders of IBM. It has withstood earthquake after earthquake. Now each day surfers park their cars right in front of the house and make their trek to the beach, down the access stairs that have been constructed. These surfers have even nicknamed my house the "history house." I'm proud of it and the role that it has played.

So here I am and Oceanside is where I will remain. I have friends from high school and I have Stan John, a companion with whom I share my life. I continue to feel blessed. And for Nancy Boyer, aka Sunbeam, when the day comes to a close I find myself looking out my window to the Pacific Ocean below. Sunbeams spread their rays across the golden west and divide into colors of orange and crimson, settling slowly into the depths of the ocean.

Yes, I have been blessed and, yes, I have also been lucky. And though I may be slowing down, the goal and the path for me remain the same: Try to live the way God wants, one day at a time. Try to have compassion and serenity for the world, and try to provide as much love to those in my life as each day permits.

CHAPTER 13

Proud to be an American
Jim Schroder

When I think back on my life I realize I've been able to do many things. I've traveled extensively, to 123 countries, and enjoyed a certain amount of freedom that most people don't have. But during these years and these travels, I've come to believe that an important aspect of what we're supposed to be doing is to help others. And if we are so fortunate to be able to affect the world in a positive way, we should do it. For me, it's about building bridges, but I'll be getting to this.

I've lived in Oceanside almost all of my life. At graduation in 1963, I know that I was just another student among the more than two hundred of us. I didn't stand out. For example, I hadn't taken on any of those roles of responsibility deemed to be so important by high school administrators. I never held an office in student council. My grades were good, but weren't considered to be fantastic, and I wasn't scoring winning touchdowns or shooting the lights out at the gym. Jim Schroder was just another student among the mix of the relative unknowns.

I'm saying this and, hopefully, making it clear that even though high school represents an important part of growing up and of life, it's not the main part. In fact, in many ways, and this is what happened with me, life in high school was just the beginning. I know that through-out school and even afterwards I had many advantages, but there are others with backgrounds such as mine, or who come from an even more advantageous family, that don't do well. Yes, I was fortunate, but from the earliest age I was able to learn from both my parents and my grandparents and use their teachings. They guided me and served as role models that even now I follow. I'll begin with my grandparents.

One grandfather came from Wales, the other from Germany. Our grandmothers were first generation born here of families that had come from Sweden and Switzerland. They came here with a purpose and with a reason. They saw America as the land of opportunity and it was here where they believed they could make a better life. Opportunities were severely restricted in their native countries, but once in the U.S. there was no stop-ping them. It was hard work, long hours and minimal pay. One of my grandfathers worked in the mines and barely survived a mine accident. The other was a farmer. They were proud folk and proud of this country, believing from the very moment they stepped off the boat in the American ethos: this is the land of opportunity. The United States had become their home.

One most important facet of their adjustment to America, and this was something that was to have a direct impact on me, was that they understood the kinds of difficulties people experienced and they were actively involved in helping their fellow man. This idea of "helping" was repeated many times. For my grandparents, they believed in hard work, be grateful for what you have, and when you're in a position to help others, do it.

And now to my parents: my dad was in the Army during World War II. He was a captain in charge of food service.

A soldier lives and dies according to the food that feeds him, and for anyone who's been out in the field you know personally how important this is. If you want a happy soldier, he needs to have good food in his belly. However, my dad's career was to change dramatically when he was injured, and this happened here in the U.S. A tank rammed the jeep he was in; he broke his back and was almost paralyzed. Prior to this injury, he had been scheduled to go to Europe, but the accident prevented this. He continued experiencing some discomfort for several years, but he always felt he was fortunate that it had not been worse. He was subsequently reassigned, throughout the east and west coasts, becoming more and more knowledgeable and expert in food service, which later influenced him to go into the restaurant business.

My mother, prior to the war and during the war, was a nurse in charge of a large medical clinic in San Diego. My parents married during the war. When the war ended, people throughout the nation were ready for change and my parents, being young and enthusiastic, wanted to break out and try something new. Taking what was a big risk, they sold their house in San Diego in preparation to begin a new business. "Why not a small restaurant?" they asked themselves, "But where?"

They drove up the coast from San Diego, looking not just for a place to start a business, but also a place where they could live and raise a family. The search extended from San Diego to Oceanside, checking out the various possibilities along the way. They ended up buying a small coffee shop in downtown Oceanside.

Why Oceanside? It was both a military community and a city that would attract tourists. It boasted of having the longest pier on the coast, and the beaches were pristine with sand that sometimes would extend a hundred yards or more out to the surf. They bought a small coffee shop and named it Marty's Coffee Shop, after my dad. It did okay, but they soon realized this coffee shop would never produce the income they believed was possible for them selves. They had dreams and were willing to pursue them.

The following year they took another risk. They bought a larger restaurant located on Hill Street, just a few hundred yards from the first coffee shop, calling it Marty's Steak House and it turned out to be a winner. Marty's Steak House became the leading steak house in Oceanside from 1947 to 1964. The restaurant business requires long hours and because of this my younger brother and I were introduced to the businesses almost as babies. This especially holds true for my brother who is four and a half years younger than me. Our parents worked while the two of us played and drew in our coloring books. At times we were permitted to do some basic things, probably causing more work for our parents than we actually performed, but the reimbursement for our efforts was excellent. We were paid in crayons. We were happy campers.

In 1953 my parents decided to take a quantum leap, a gamble that would either make or break them; in many ways it was a roll of the dice. (If you're going to be success-ful, you have to be willing to take some risks.) The San Luis Rey Valley, located just outside of Oceanside, was a kind of no man's land, or better yet a no businessman's land. It consisted mostly of a dry riverbed where the principle crop was lima beans. The roads extending through this valley were adequate, for the limited use they received and there were but three basic choices. One choice was to the back gate at Camp Pendleton, which was used pri-marily by Marines. Another choice led to the old Mission San Luis Rey, used primarily for Sunday services or field trips from the various elementary schools. And the third choice was to take the road to Highway 395 and head off to the Mojave Desert, definitely a "no man's land".

So in the midst of this dry riverbed, what crazy scheme did my parents come up with? They purchased thirteen acres and built a fancy restaurant in the middle of lima bean heaven. The doubters and the naysayers came out in droves. "You're going to be broke within three months," said friends and acquaintances. (More than ninety-five percent of the people who go into the restaurant business are unsuccessful.) Only to be followed by, "No one goes out there. It's away from the beach and downtown. Are you sure you really want to do this?" And then there were those who had been influenced by modern day psychology and the Sigmund Freud approach: "Are the two of you out of your minds? You need to see a psychologist."

Marty's Valley Inn opened in February 17th, 1955, and became the first business in the overall deserted landscape. It was built to be a fancy dinner house with cocktails and dancing, coat and tie required. Six months later that coat and tie requirement was junked for the casualness and more laid-back atmosphere of the beach and of Oceanside.

It began by seating 125 and grew to 500. The hotel Best Western and Marty's Valley Inn began in 1960 with 39 rooms and grew to 111 rooms and convention facilities for 200. As I think back to my childhood, adolescence, and to my early adulthood, my experiences at this restaurant and hotel were something extraordinaire. Movies stars: Lucille Ball and Desi Arnaz made Marty's a getaway place on their way to Del Mar. Johnny Weissmuller of Tarzan fame and an Olympic swimmer made frequent visits. It was not uncommon for Johnny to let out his renowned Tarzan yell late in the evenings, capping off what was just another day at the Inn. Johnny also taught my younger brother, who was only six or seven at the time, to swim. We had the Andrew Sisters--"Boogie Woogie Bugle Boy of Company B." Debbie Reynolds, part of the Hollywood throng, along with the future President of the United States, Ronald Reagan, all paid us visits. This one-time bean field turned restaurant provided a safety net for the stars away from Tinsel Town, where they could relax, golf in the nearby golf courses, and enjoy themselves, while I was taking it all in. Later, during the sixties, seventies, and eighties, Marty's Valley Inn became a kind of microcosm of society, representing in its own way some of the most important issues with which the nation was dealing.

But before going into the various societal issues that were being partially played out at the Inn, which will add an important historical perspective to my story, I first need to return to my formative years. I was born in San Diego and came to Oceanside when I was six weeks old. I started kindergarten at Ditmar Street School and was one of the youngest in the class, having been born January 20th, 1946, being eligible by just eleven days. Throughout these elementary years, I played a kind of musical chairs with schools: Nevada Street, Horn Street, and then back to Ditmar. Fortunately, even with these changes I was always able to walk to school. The baby boom, which officially began in 1946, was having its first impact as I started my elementary education, causing my friends and I to traipse off to these unexpected yearly locations. Horn Street School, and it was truly the novel one of the bunch, opened for just one year and then closed its doors forever, but no one was surprised. It was located on the high school campus.

After these many changes in elementary school, another change seemed somewhat insignificant as I matriculated to the school on the distant hill, Jefferson

Junior High School. I, along with my friends, for the first time had to ride the bus. For the most part, and you will see why I am qualifying this, I enjoyed Jefferson, but then one day I was to have one of the strangest experiences of my life. (I'm telling this because it is also a good example of how education and what teachers could do have changed over these past years.)

I was picking up attendance rosters from the various rooms. After all, assisting at the attendance office was an excellent way to get out of class and I cherished the freedom it allowed. I had done this collection of rosters previously and believe that it's quite possible that on this day I might have been just a little lax. Possibly I could have been roaming around or simply sitting down, but I arrived at the girls' gym much later than was expected.

The girls' PE teacher, and she had a reputation of being rather bellicose and somewhat irrational, was in one of her bad moods. She grabbed me by my arm and hauled me toward the girls' locker room. The girls' P.E. classes were still out on the field. With a grip as tight as a vice, she thrust me through the doors and to the showers. I think several others also followed. She then proceeded to throw me on the ground, covering my face with towels. And with a foot planted firmly on my head, so that I had no possibility of escape, she turned on the showers. "You'll never do this again," she shouted as water poured down upon me.

I was then set free, wet and confused, to resume my duty of returning the rosters to the attendance office. (Can you imagine something like this happening today?) Strange? Yes! Even at the time I could hardly believe what I had just experienced, but interestingly enough I shrugged it all off. I think I even laughed to myself, feeling a sense of pride about how well I had handled this out of the ordinary experience. This event continued to be my secret and I would tell no one, but I could walk tall, knowing that this P.E. teacher hadn't gotten the best of me. I believe how I emotionally handled this was an indication of my inner ability to emotionally adjust to whatever might come my way. Junior high school ended and I was off to high school.

In 1959, living but four blocks from the campus, I started Oceanside High School. My freshman year I went out for track, competing in a variety of events. I was small, light and fast, a jack-of-all-trades, master-of-none. Track was a positive experience, but this one-year comprised my total high school athletic career. Starting my sophomore year, everyday at three o'clock I began a separate life and had a totally different persona: morning time high school student, afternoons and evenings responsible and hard working young adult. The two were interesting contrasts, but through these combined experiences I believe I was able to enjoy the best of both worlds.

Marty's Valley Inn, as I already stated, had become Oceanside's happening place and I, this young and effervescent teenager, was cast in the middle of an ongoing cornucopia of famous people, newspapers from faraway lands, and out-of-the-blue, ear drum busting Tarzan yells. And all the time my mind was being tantalized with the prospect of travel, adventure, and of a yet to be experienced, but exciting world. I knew before graduation that my life was destined to be something out of the ordinary, with dreams of it approaching the spectacular. I envisioned myself visiting foreign countries, socializing with the rich and famous... as well as the common folk, experiencing different cultures, and that somewhere in this mix I would even learn a foreign language. "Oh," I thought to myself, "If only high school would end so I could get on *with my life.*" But I had to wait, and wait, and wait. In the meantime there were two teachers that I enjoyed and who inadvertently reinforced my secret fantasy.

One was Mrs. Saxon, my English teacher. She took her subject seriously...don't all English teachers, but what maintained my interest and enthusiasm was not the subject she taught, but her love for the world and what it had to offer. "See the world," she encouraged. She inspired, "Get away from the limited and myopic view Oceanside provides." Here was this diminutive, middle-aged, and slightly rotund lady talking my language, all the while whetting my appetite for what I knew would surely be my destiny.

The other, and quite unexpected source of reinforcement came from Mr. Troy, my advanced math teacher. Now math certainly wasn't my favorite subject, but he taught me to think creatively, outside of the box. Advanced math was a struggle, but thinking creatively and outside the box seemed to fit into my scheme of doing things. It served to reinforce these plans of travel, independence and survival. By the end of my senior year I was ready.

Then on Monday, almost immediately after we returned from graduation night, I put my plans into action. With ticket in hand, my destination was Europe. London was my first stop; I didn't know a soul. One day I was a wet-behind-the-ears high school student and the next I was making my way in a soon-to-be-discovered world. Did I know what I was doing? Probably not, but I had my itinerary. I would do X, Y and Z. I found myself in places that we'd studied in school: Westminster Abby, the Eiffel Tower, and the Coliseum. I traveled to Wales and walked the same streets that my grandfather walked before the turn of century. It gave me chills. What was life like for him? And I knew that no one in my immediate family had ever been off the continental United States, but there I was. Every corner had something new, exciting and challenging. And through all of this, though I was only seventeen, I proved to myself that I could survive, no matter where I was or in what situation I might find myself. I ended up spending two months and as a result I would never be the same. Just as the caterpillar goes through a metamorphosis, I was in the midst of a dramatic change. Then the money ran out.

I flew back to the United States, landed in New York and visited the various sights, and then traveled to Boston and Washington D.C. It was 1963 and this was a time when racial tensions were running on high. In Washington D.C., I got caught in a race riot. People were fighting and knocking each other down. My taxi driver, an African-American, told me that it was very dangerous and that I'd better find a safe place. (Remember also that in1965 there were six days of riots in Watts.) He dropped me off at a Greyhound Bus Station, warning me to hide, while the police with batons in hand, battled an angry and threatening mob. I took refuge in the men's bathroom, waiting it out in one of the stalls, all the while listening to the discordant clashes outside. Little did I know that the United States was about to enter one of its darkest periods: the Vietnam War, race riots, drugs, student protests, and a total re-thinking of our values.

It took me several more weeks before I returned to Oceanside, but once back I felt different. In fact, everyone told me I had changed. I was not the same and I knew they were right. College was up next.

I began at San Diego State, living not too far from the university with my grandparents. After all, it was the closest, the cheapest, the most logical, and where many of my friends were destined, but San Diego State and being an

Aztec was not my fate. Whatever it was that had driven me to go to Europe—perhaps Gypsy blood lurking covertly in my genealogy—had again kicked in. I would attend a different college each year, making sure that I carried a sufficient number of classes. After four years and four colleges, I had two degrees from Chapman University: one in Economics and the other in Business Administration.

But the draft and the Army's call for warm bodies, with their destination of Vietnam, had me in their sights. The day came when I found myself in Los Angeles at their central locale for Army inductees. Hundreds of us were being put through the Army physical. We were ushered along, step-by-step, lining up here and proceeding to a variety of different stations, all of which led to the culmination of being sworn in. Finally, when I'd proceed through all of the stations, I stood waiting with the rest, only to find myself rejected… high blood pressure. (I was later able to control it without medication, but at this point in my life I did have a serious problem.)

There would be no military, no basic training, no Vietnam for me. International business, providing the additional enticement of adventure and travel, was to be my calling, at least that's what I envisioned, but the world has a way of intervening and upsetting even the best-made plans. After graduation, I returned to temporarily help out with my parent's business. One year passed, then two and three, while the business grew and grew. Oceanside was where I would remain and this brings me back to Marty's Valley Inn and the important role that it played.

The Vietnam War was at its height with almost five hundred thousand soldiers in South East Asia. While our troops were being killed, here in the U.S. we were having demonstrations against the war. Joan Baez, Jane Fonda, Pete Seeger, and many others were at the center of these protests. In Oceanside and at Marty's Valley Inn, we had families of the Marines and Navy staying with us, and many times their sons, husbands, boyfriends, or just friends were going to Vietnam and getting wounded or even killed. Customers, out of a respect and pride for what these men were doing, frequently asked for the checks of these soldiers and sailors. Even now when I think about this I become emotional. At the apogee of this war, Marty's Valley Inn was nicknamed Command Post West (CP West) by the military.

With friends and classmates, as well as many others suffering the extreme effects of this war, the least I could do was to provide them with my emotional support, a support that I continue to offer. Camp Pendleton and Oceanside are the first to directly experience the effects of combat situations. In 2010, I read that we recently had thirteen Marines killed in one week from the conflict in Afghanistan.

Marty's Valley Inn, primarily because of its location, also ended up playing an important role with President Nixon and the Western White House, located in San Clemente. Secret service men would helicopter into the nearby airport and get their lodging. Marty's Valley Inn, though officially unknown and unrecognized by politicians and the military alike, throughout these years provided a most important and needed service.

And, interestingly enough, along with these official types of visits, we would also have private helicopters landing directly adjacent to the Inn. And then we could have people riding horses up to the restaurant, tying them off at a large outdoor tree and joining us for a breakfast of bacon, eggs and coffee. It was an amazing combination of both the past and present occurring at the same time.

Anyway, after completing my college education, I continued working in the business, eventually taking over the reigns, but my wanderlust and desire to see the world remained. In 1973, I traveled to Yugoslavia. I was part of a small group and we'd actually visited several other countries, prior to going to Yugoslavia, where I decided to stay on for several days. The police, unannounced and without provocation, came to my room and searched me. They accused me of being a spy, telling me I couldn't leave the country. I was under what was termed "country arrest" and my exiting plane tickets were cancelled. Police followed me. Fortunately, I learned that there was a flight leaving the country and that a group of Romanians was going to be on it. Panic-stricken and knowing that this was my only chance to get out; I forced my way into this group. I hugged to the middle and my heart raced. I kept low so that I couldn't be recognized, all the while sweating as though I'd been running a marathon. When the plane finally landed in Rome I breathed a welcome sign of relief, knowing that I was most fortunate to make my escape.

I was alive, safe, and wiser. Upon my return to Oceanside, I had a better appreciation of the freedoms we enjoy in this country and my wanderlust abated, though it would again return. I threw myself into the center of the business; at one point we had almost three hundred employees, including two Burger Kings in San Diego. Five years later my gypsy blood again kicked in and it was to time to journey back into the world. Unfortunately, I soon found myself in what I consider to be perhaps the most dangerous, and then the most fortuitous time of my life.

It was 1978 and the trip began with me going to Columbia. In Bogotá, I was shot at. It did not take much deep thinking on my part as I quickly decided this was not a country for me. I proceeded to Paraguay where I found myself going from the frying pan into the fire. It all began as a peaceful Saturday evening when I went for a stroll around the central plaza of Asuncion, the capitol. A crowd had gathered to watch a wedding in the main cathedral and I stood with them. Someone asked me the time in Spanish. I showed them my watch, not saying anything. All of a sudden police came up from behind, throwing me to the ground. They pointed their guns into my body, demanding my passport. I lay motionless on the ground.

"I don't have it," I told them and I didn't. It actually was at the airport. "It's at the hotel," I responded, out of a deep sense of fear.

I was then taken to my hotel. When I got there I yelled at the top of my lungs, "Help, I'm an American. I'm an American. I have been arrested. Call the American Embassy."

Another American came over to find out what was going on and he was cold-cocked and knocked unconscious. Then I was taken to jail where the guards tried to plant drugs on me. This was unsuccessful and once again I found myself being accused of spying. (I believe that accusing someone of spying, such as what happened in Iran to several young Americans, is difficult to disprove and gives the authorities permission to proceed in any way they desire.) So there I was in jail and it was the middle of the night. I knew I had no freedoms and these authorities could do whatever they wanted. Then an unknown voice called out: "Are you Jim Schroder?" I replied I was. A guard unlocked the cell and disappeared. This stranger in a low voice instructed: "Follow me." I did as I was told, fearful now of being killed as I tried to escape. Somehow

I felt that death might be the better choice over the dark jail in which I had been placed.

It turned out this person was from the Swiss Embassy and he took me to the airport, placing me on a plane. I was Argentina bound and would now be safe, but was also aware that at this time Argentina was yet another country with political strife and police rule.

I was getting a first-hand, real life education in what it's like in these despotic countries where people have no freedoms. And I know now that because of everything that I have seen and personally experienced, I have a deep appreciation of the United States and of our system of government. Through the reality of these other countries of the world, I came to understand what we mean by freedom. We can be politically active without fear of reprisals. The words "God Bless America" have become very dear to me, and the older I've gotten the more meaningful they've become.

Once I returned to Oceanside, happy to be alive and away from the oppression and despotic policies, my attention returned to the business. In 1989, after more than forty-five years of marriage, my mother passed away. My father lived for another nine years, but these years were not easy for him. Not only had he lost his wife, but he had also lost his business companion and associate. He was in a bad car accident and he made the decision that he should no longer drive. How would he manage? The next thing I knew he'd hired a chauffeur. Nothing was going to stop him from going on with his life and being productive. In 1998, he was honored as the oldest working Best Western owner in the world by Best Western International in Las Vegas. Three weeks later he passed away. There were eleven hundred people at his funeral.

I grew up in the restaurant and hotel business, having the opportunity to learn as I went along. I learned early that it takes hard work and long hours, and that the more people you know the better. I took the family lead in this area and became involved in networking. It was social and it was good for business, but soon I realized it was something more. These organizations serve a duel purpose: business contacts and networking, and they reach out to help people. Through various organizations, directly and indirectly I've been involved with hundreds and even thousands of people, all providing valuable services to others. There is not the space to go into everything that I've been involved with, but I will mention a few that have been most important to me.

We gave eight hundred bicycles to children in Tijuana and Ensenada. We've helped orphanages in Mexico. I've served as a liaison between the United States and Mexico. I became a fluent Spanish speaker, one of my earliest goals. I've been able to use these Spanish skills as I've translated for American doctors who provide care to some of the most crippled and handicapped of Mexican children, all of which was done through Shriner's Hospital. And along the way I was honored by the President of Mexico, Salinas de Gortari. I am most proud of this because it represented the combined efforts of so many of us working together to provide for the needs of the Mexican people.

When I was forty-five I was chosen to be group leader to Argentina and Uruguay, a project through the Rotary Clubs of San Diego and Imperial Counties. It was the first coed team to go international. Throughout this trip, we stayed with Rotarians and their families in both countries. As a group we were on TV frequently and we also met with political leaders. What was most significant were the number of friendships that developed and the variety of projects that we were able to complete. It truly was building bridges between countries. These friendships continue today.

But now I need to return to Oceanside and to one of the most memorable experiences of my life. In 1991, I was President of the Oceanside of Commerce. The Chamber and the City of Oceanside planned a day of recognition, April 27, 1991, for the servicemen of the Marines and the Navy. I was the co-chairman for this activity and it was titled, "Proud to be an American Day." We would welcome home the returning Marines and Navy from Kuwait, after the liberation of Kuwait in what was termed "Operation Desert Storm." There were three thousand civilian volunteers, along with the ten thousand Marines who participated in this parade. The throng of ten thousand came marching down Hill Street in their cameys (their camouflaged fatigues) and it was a most impressive sight.

This was one of the first Welcome Home celebrations in the United States commemorating the return of our military from the Mid-East. (It generated both national and international news.) As the Marines marched in unison down the street and as the Marine band led the way, something spontaneous happened that none of us will ever forget. More than three hundred Vietnam veterans joined in. The streets were ten deep on each side with spectators as these Marines and veterans marched by. People screamed to the top of their lungs: "Thank you, thank you."

This unanticipated joint parading of soldiers, those of the present with those of the past, brought tears to all of our eyes. And to top it all off, "Proud to be an American," by Lee Greenwood played loud and clear. Yes, I've grown up in Oceanside and over the years I've traveled throughout the world, but I truly am proud to be an American and this was one of my proudest moments.

So here I am and here I remain. I've had some amazing experiences and am not sure how or why I made it this far. I could of, should of, been killed several times. I've also been lost at sea in a hurricane and just missed being on a plane that crashed, killing everyone aboard. I believe that God has somehow pulled me through, and it is because of Him that I'm still here. So it is with His grace that I continue to be involved in a variety of activities and organizations, and it is with His grace that I can continue to provide any assistance to others that I can. But through these last almost fifty years, I know that this Class of 1963 is special and I'm fortunate to be a part of it. We've lived through wars, the drug culture, the sexual revolution, women's liberation, recessions and much more. This Class of ours has accomplished so many incredible things and as we move into our more advanced years,

We can say with pride,

That we're the class of 1963,

From Oceanside

Jim Schroder has been involved with a number of organizations over the past forty years, both locally and internationally. This includes organizations in Oceanside, California, throughout the nation, Argentina, Japan and Mexico. He has consistently taken on leadership roles, frequently as the organization's president. He is the only American to have served on the Tijuana Chamber of Commerce Board, which he did for a number of years. He has coordinated projects through Rotary International with Argentina and the Oceanside Rotarians. He has served as a liaison between Mexico, Argentina, Europe, and Japan. Jim Schroder has also worked tirelessly with mayors and leaders in numerous cities and countries. Channel 10 in San Diego honored him with their

Leadership Award, Oceanside Chamber of Commerce selected him as Business Person of the year, KOCT television presented an hour-long program showcasing the fine work he has done. And in 2011 Jim was inducted in the Oceanside High School's Hall of Fame. Jim walks his talk. He continues to build bridges across nations and firmly believes in the words, "Friendship moves the world".

CHAPTER 14

The Ten Principles for Happiness

These thirteen graduates from Oceanside High School's class of 1963 are all at least sixty-five years of age, and it is approximately fifty years since their graduation. As a group they have proven themselves to be exemplary in dealing with life and its many challenges, both positive and negative. Each has experienced a variety of difficulties and setbacks, but through it all they have successfully adapted, adjusted, survived, and in their own individual ways they have even thrived. These ten principles, which have been developed from their life stories and from knowledge they have gained over their sixty-five plus years, provide the guidelines for successfully dealing with whatever life brings to each of us, as well as finding happiness along life's ongoing journey.

The Ten Principles:

1. Maintain a positive outlook on life. Even though each of these graduates has experienced their fair share of problems and setbacks, they don't tend to look at these problems or setbacks in a negative fashion. They take the negative, those disappointments and obstacles, and have both learned and grown from these experiences. In a sense, they've turned what could be considered as a negative into a positive. "Turn lemons into lemonade," was a comment that several specifically made. And they highlighted this approach by continually focusing their attention and their lives on seeing the good.

2. Live in the present! Enjoy as much as you can from each day. Take time to laugh and retain your sense of humor, and this can only occur by living in the here and now. Each day is special and unique and needs to be lived and enjoyed. Happiness can only be experienced in the present moment. These graduates are concerned about making the most of each day and living that day in the manner by which it can be said to be truly precious.

3. Connection with God. This spiritual connection is important to most within this group. It could be a connection with Jesus Christ, through traditional churches and religion, or through a more non-traditional approach. But there seems to be a trust in this spiritual presence as well as a personal recognition that God answers prayers, though not always the way we had thought. Several of these graduates have made personal decisions and commitments that God is to be the primary focus of their lives. Most of them try to live in line with God's principles and they try to do this on a daily basis.

4. Be courageous and live life your way. They all talked about having the courage to confront life head on and not to back away from its many challenges. They consider themselves as risk takers, but they are not reckless in taking these risks. All are concerned about success and strive for it, but they are not distraught when what might be termed "failure" occurs. In fact, what many people would define as failure would most likely be described by them as "an unsuccessful attempt." In living life their way, it is important for them to use those many talents and abilities that each has been given. This means getting an education, though not necessarily a college education, and proceeding along those areas that are the most in line with their abilities.

5. Happiness is on the inside. This is a consistent statement that serves to define these individuals. It's not the external, material world that brings them happiness. It is not the "shop until you drop scenario," or the "keep up with the Jones," but rather happiness emanates from inside and from the central core of their being. This inner state of happiness is always maintained and protected, and it radiates outwardly to whatever they may be doing.

6. Compassion for others. Compassion is a deep feeling for others and empathy is a most important aspect of this. These graduates feel deeply for what others may be experiencing. As a group, however, their sentiments extend beyond what would be just an internal feeling of empathy or compassion. They are willing to take an active stance to affect the world in a positive way and to take measures that will directly impact and help others. Their actions are not done for any monetary reward or gain, or for any external recognition, but from this inner state of compassion for their fellow man.

7. Have friends and maintain friendships. They are all actively involved in reaching out to their friends, loved ones, and to others they've met along this journey of life. Some have maintained friendships with high school teachers or other teachers from the past; but an important commonality is that they're not afraid to make direct contact with others. The Internet is important as well as all other forms of communication in maintaining these friendships.

8. Self-honesty/self-responsibility. They don't get into the blame game and are very honest with themselves. In fact, self-honesty is one of their most important characteristics. This self-honesty and self-responsibility are central in how they relate to others, themselves, and to life. Self-honesty leads directly to honesty in how they relate to the world. In understanding this self-honesty, they try to avoid feeling sorry for themselves when things don't go their way. When things happen that they don't like, so what! Instead of blaming others when something unsettling happens, they take the self-responsibility needed to get out of the quagmire or unfortunate situation in which they've somehow become entangled.

9. Communication. Communication comes from the heart to the heart. Egos that want to prove themselves, or are emotionally predisposed to the concept of "winning at any cost" are not the way they function. Communication is listening, sharing, and reaching a middle ground where both parties find a resolution that is acceptable. It means having the capacity to both give and receive. In marriage, effective communication is demonstrated by their willingness and ability to subjugate their immediate needs for the overall benefit of the relationship. Another aspect of communication is their ability to learn from respected people around them. They are able to make those internal judgments that enable them to make positive changes and to do so without experiencing excessive resistance to such change. They are good listeners.

10. Acceptance of themselves and others. These gradu-ates are survivors and understand imperfections, both of themselves and of others. They don't harbor grudges and actively strive to avoid or reduce animosity. If a marriage breaks up, their task is to reduce the emotional pain that is sure to result, and they take an active role for the well being of their children. These graduates accept them-selves as they are, realizing their strengths as well as their weaknesses. They have friends of many different races and cultures.

These are the ten principles by which these gradu-ates have survived and found happiness and success along the way. Life is meant to be fun and enjoyed each and every day, and this is achieved through an active and courageous approach. They live in the present. Communication and honesty form their core as they relate in both a giving and receiving manner. All, in one form or another, are actively involved in helping others. And when the going gets tough, their personal relation-ship with God helps to pull them through.

For these graduates of Oceanside High School's class of 1963, both growing older and life itself are part of the process. And when they look at themselves and what they've experienced, "it's been the journey, not any indi-vidual goal, that has been important."

Yes, an amazing amount of time has passed since their high school graduation in 1963. 2013 will mark half a century. But each of these graduates, and this has been through the Vietnam War, the draft, college, successes and defeats, financial woes, loves and sorrows, has devel-oped patterns for living and finding happiness that truly have made their lives worth living.

ABOUT THE AUTHOR

Richard (Dick) Selby graduated with Oceanside High School's class of 1963 and after graduation matriculated to the nearby community college. At this time it was known as Oceanside-Carlsbad Junior College, but during his sophomore year the campus moved away from the high school where it was located and it also changed it's name. It became known as Mira Costa College and Dick was among Mira Costa College's first graduates. In 1965, during his sophomore year, Dick went out for Mira Costa's track team and became the top javelin thrower in the state of California. He then transferred to UCLA where he received a full athletic scholarship. In 1966, he became an All-American, school record holder, and he was a member of the 1966 UCLA National Championship Track Team.

In 1970, Dick began working for the Los Angeles Unified School District. He worked in the Los Angeles Unified School District for 34 years, working as a teacher, counselor, and more than 20 years as a school psychologist. With more than 400 school psychologists in the district, twice Dick was honored as a "School Psychologist of the Year," an award presented by his fellow school psychologists. Dick worked seventeen years at Garfield High School, a school made famous by Jaime Escalante and the movie "Stand and Deliver." He has written a book about his experiences at Garfield and with the Los Angeles Unified School

District. It is titled *A School Psychologist in East L.A.* It can be purchased through Amazon.com

In 1984, Dick took up beach volleyball and has played on a team with the late Wilt Chamberlain. Aside from basketball, Wilt Chamberlain loved beach volleyball. Dick has also teamed up at various times with Butch May, a former Olympian and the father of Olympic champion Misty May-Trainer, and Bob Vogelsang, credited with developing the jump serve. Dick and Butch twice won the California State Masters' Championship at Manhattan Beach, and Bob Vogelsang and Dick won the informal National Masters' Championships at Santa Barbara.

Dick has made thirteen trips to India and is a follower of the now deceased Sri Sathya Sai Baba who died on April 24th, 2011. Sai Baba's principles of love, peace, truth, right action, and non-violence are principles that Dick has incorporated into his life. Dick has written three books about his experiences with Sai Baba, all of which have been published in India.

Made in the USA
San Bernardino, CA
27 July 2016